Anxiety Therapy

for Men

Heal Yourself in 21 Days

ISBN 978-93-343-1774-9

Publishing Year 2025

Anxiety Therapy

for Men

Heal Yourself in 21 Days

ABHIJIT SHARMA

About the Author & Acknowledgements

I was born and raised in the beautiful states of Assam and Meghalaya, India. My father was a banker, and my mother was the daughter of an NRI doctor. Unfortunately, my parents separated during my early childhood, and my mother never came to see me again. My father, busy with his career, would occasionally visit, I lived mostly in hostels or rented accommodations. During this time, my relatives showed little interest in taking responsibility for me, leaving me to face a lonely, unwanted existence. This led me to become a victim of anxiety and depression.

Throughout my life, I have searched tirelessly for happiness. I immersed myself in research, reading around 700 books on the subject. Eventually, I uncovered the secrets to happiness, and by applying them to my life, I was able to transform my life completely. The exercises shared in this book have been integral to my personal journey. Today, I am a rich and successful businessman, surrounded by friends, well-wishers, and the respect of my relatives, who now seek my advice.

I am deeply grateful to everyone who has come into my life, as each person has taught me invaluable lessons. I would like to express my heartfelt thanks to Dr. Deepak Kelkar and Dr. Manish Sethi Jain, whose participation in the transformative Magic workshop was pivotal to my growth. I am also indebted to my mentor, Mr. Pradeep Kumar, whose guidance inspired me to read regularly. A special thank you to my wonderful wife, Papari, who has taught me countless lessons, and to my two amazing children, Dhun and Jiu, for bringing so much joy into my life.

I am eternally grateful to my friends, relatives, in-laws for their unwavering love and support. Lastly, I thank God and the beauty of nature for helping me train my brain to embrace happiness in any circumstance.

Thank you, thank you, thank you.

Abhijit Sharma

Contents

Introduction:

A Man's Guide to Reclaiming Peace, Strength, and Clarity

Introduction: A Man's Guide to Reclaiming Peace, Strength, and Clarity

"You don't have to be fearless to be strong. You just have to show up for yourself, even when it's hard."
– Anonymous

Why This Book Exists

If you're reading this, chances are you've been battling anxiety — silently, privately, maybe even in denial. You've felt the racing thoughts, the tight chest, the constant edge like something's about to go wrong. Maybe you've tried to push it down, work through it, ignore it — because that's what you were taught.

As men, we're often raised to **be strong, stay quiet, and tough it out.** But anxiety doesn't care about masculinity. It sneaks in, wraps itself around your mind and body, and makes you question your worth, your safety, and your power.

This book is your space to drop the armor — and **start healing**.

You don't have to fix everything overnight. You don't have to pretend to be okay.

What you do need is a **plan**, a **toolbox**, and the **courage to show up for yourself** — one day at a time.

What This Book Will Do for You

Anxiety Healing for Men: Heal Yourself in 21 Days is not a fluffy, overcomplicated self-help book. It's a straightforward, no-nonsense guide designed for men who want results. Inside, you'll find:

- **Proven techniques** to reduce anxiety naturally — no judgment, no fluff.
- **Daily lessons** that blend science, psychology, and practical exercises.
- **Mindset shifts** that help you stop over thinking and start acting.
- **Stories and examples** from real men who've faced anxiety and reclaimed control.
- **Tools you can actually use** — breathing, journaling, reframing, boundaries, and more.

This isn't about perfection — it's about **progress**.

What Anxiety Is — And Isn't

Anxiety is not weakness. It's not something "wrong" with you. It's a biological response that got stuck in overdrive.

When your brain perceives danger (even emotional danger), it triggers the fight-or-flight system. That's great if you're being chased by a bear — not so great when you're lying in bed trying to sleep.

Anxiety becomes a problem when it starts running your life. You avoid people. You can't focus. Your chest feels tight all the time. You lose sleep, lose patience, and maybe even lose hope.

But here's the truth: anxiety can be managed. You can learn to regulate your nervous system, challenge your thoughts, and build mental strength.

Why 21 Days?

Studies show that it takes **21 days to begin forming a new habit**. When you practice intentional actions daily, you literally **rewire your brain**.

This program is built on that principle.

Each day, you'll tackle one core element of anxiety — from thought patterns to triggers to physical grounding tools. You'll build on what you learned the day before. It's not random — it's a carefully crafted journey from chaos to clarity.

By Day 21, you won't just feel different — **you'll be different.**

How to Use This Book

You don't need to read the whole thing at once. In fact, you shouldn't.

Each chapter represents **one day** of the healing process. Here's how to make the most of it:

1. **Read one chapter per day** — ideally in the morning or evening when your mind is calm.
2. **Do the exercises** — this isn't just theory. Healing happens in action.
3. **Use the journal prompts** — writing helps process emotions and reveal patterns.
4. **Repeat what works for you** — some tools will click more than others. That's okay.
5. **Don't skip hard days** — those are the ones that transform you most.

Keep a notebook or journal nearby. You'll want to track your progress, insights, and any moments of breakthrough.

When to Seek Help

This book is a self-help tool — but it's not a substitute for professional therapy, medication, or crisis intervention. If your anxiety is severe or includes panic attacks, trauma flashbacks, or thoughts of self-harm, please reach out to a licensed therapist or counselor.

Healing takes bravery — and sometimes that means asking for help.

There's no shame in that. In fact, it's one of the strongest moves you can make.

What You'll Learn Over the Next 21 Days

Here's a preview of the journey ahead:

Week 1 – Understanding and Grounding

- Learn what's happening in your brain and body.
- Discover your anxiety triggers.
- Master breathing and calming techniques.

Week 2 – Tools for Transformation

- Build resilience through journaling, mindfulness, and boundaries.

- Start shifting your thoughts, your habits, and your perspective.

Week 3 – Empowerment and Growth

- Reclaim confidence.
- Let go of perfectionism.
- Design a life that supports your peace.

By the end, you'll have a **toolkit for life.**

Final Words Before You Begin

If no one's told you this lately: **you're doing the right thing.**

Reading this book, taking this step, choosing to heal — this is **real strength.**

You don't have to live in a state of tension. You don't have to carry it alone. You can learn to feel safe in your own mind and body again.

All it takes is one day at a time.

Let's begin.

Part I:

Foundations of Healing

(Days 1-7)

Understanding and Grounding

Day 1: Facing the Truth About Anxiety

"You don't have to control your thoughts. You just have to stop letting them control you." – Dan Millman

When the Storm Has No Name

Meera was 28 when the storm hit. Not the kind with thunder and lightning. The storm was silent. Invisible. But it shook her entire world.

She was sitting at her desk at work, typing an email, when suddenly her chest tightened. Her heart galloped like a racehorse. She couldn't catch her breath. Her hands trembled, and a wave of dizziness flushed through her body. She felt like she was dying — or going crazy.

But there was no visible danger. Just silence and a buzzing monitor.

She called a friend in tears and ended up in the emergency room. The doctors told her something that didn't make sense at the time:

"You had a panic attack."

That was the beginning of Meera's journey — one that many of us walk without knowing its name.

Anxiety.

It disguises itself as over thinking, perfectionism, emotional exhaustion, unexplained dread, and sudden overwhelm. It's a shape-shifter that hides in the mind, body, and even behavior.

But once you name the storm, you can begin to navigate it.

What Is Anxiety?

Anxiety is your body's natural alarm system. It evolved to keep us alive. When danger was near — say, a lion in the bushes — our body needed to respond instantly: adrenaline, faster heartbeat, sharp focus, tense muscles.

That ancient system still lives in us. But today's "lions" are often not real lions — they're:

Overdue bills ,Relationship conflict, Social judgment, Fear of failure, A childhood wound triggered etc

In anxiety, the amygdala (your brain's fear center) misfires. It perceives something as dangerous — even when it may not be — and kicks off the same fight-or-flight response.

This is why anxiety feels physical: racing heart, short breath, stomach pain, muscle tension, dizziness.

But it's also emotional and mental: worry, dread, obsessing over what-ifs, anticipating the worst.

Common Symptoms of Anxiety:

Rapid heartbeat or chest tightness

Feeling restless, keyed-up, or on edge

Difficulty concentrating or sleeping

Constant worry about the future

Avoiding situations that cause fear

Feeling like you're "losing control"

Why You Must Understand It

Healing begins with awareness. You cannot heal something you don't understand or acknowledge. That's why Day 1 isn't about fixing anxiety — it's about recognizing it without shame.

Most people spend years misinterpreting their anxiety as weakness, over-sensitivity, or personal failure. But anxiety is not a flaw. It's a signal.

You wouldn't be mad at a fire alarm for going off. You'd check if something's burning.

Understanding your anxiety is the equivalent of checking the smoke detector. Is it real danger — or a false alarm?

Once you know that, you're no longer a victim. You're in charge.

Your Relationship with Anxiety

What if you stopped fighting anxiety and got curious instead?

> "What's trying to protect me right now?"

That simple question can turn fear into self-compassion.

Your anxiety isn't your enemy. It's a misguided bodyguard — trying to protect you using outdated tools. It might be protecting a 10-year-old version of you who learned to be quiet, careful, or hyper-alert because that felt safer.

But you're not that child anymore.

Story: A Conversation with Anxiety

Here's a simple visual story to reflect on.

Imagine anxiety as a small creature that lives inside your chest. Not evil. Just nervous. It wakes up every time it hears something that reminds it of past hurt.

When your boss criticizes you — it panics. When someone doesn't reply — it fears rejection. When plans change — it spirals.

Now picture yourself sitting down with this creature, not to yell at it, but to ask:

> "Hey, what are you afraid of?"

That's the beginning of emotional mastery. You don't control anxiety by force — you tame it through understanding, compassion, and new tools.

Tools for Day 1

****Daily Exercises and Solutions****

Here are four practical tools to manage anxiety:

01. Anxiety Inventory (Self-Reflection)

Take 15 minutes to write answers to these questions:

- **When do I feel most anxious?** (Mornings? At work? Before bed?)

- **What do I fear will happen?** (Example: "I'll fail the exam and disappoint everyone.")

- **How do I react?** (Do you isolate yourself? Overwork? Binge-watch TV?)

- **What have I avoided because of anxiety?** (A social event? A tough conversation?)

***Why this works**:* Writing helps you spot patterns. You might realize, "I always feel anxious after scrolling social media," or "My fear of failure comes from childhood." Revisit your answers after a few weeks to see progress.

02. 5-4-3-2-1 Grounding Method****

When your mind races, this exercise brings you back to the present:

1. **5 things you see**: A lamp, a tree outside, a coffee mug.

2. **4 things you can feel**: Your socks, the chair beneath you, a breeze, your phone in your hand.

3. **3 things you hear**: Birds chirping, a clock ticking, your breath.

4. **2 things you smell**: Coffee, laundry detergent.

5. **1 thing you taste**: Gum, toothpaste, or a sip of water.

***Why this works**:* Anxiety often focuses on the future ("What if…?"). Grounding uses your senses to anchor you in the *now*, which calms your nervous system.

03. "Name It to Tame It" Method**

When anxiety hits, say out loud or write:

"Right now, I'm feeling anxious. That's okay. I am safe, and this feeling will pass."

***Why this works**:* Labeling emotions reduces their power. Studies show that naming anxiety activates the logical part of your brain, slowing down the "panic mode" in your emotional brain.

04. Create a Safe Space**

Designate a cozy corner in your home for calm moments. Include:

- A soft blanket or pillow.

- A calming scent (lavender candle, eucalyptus oil).

- A comforting object (a smooth stone, family photo, or favorite book).

- A journal to jot down thoughts.

Spend 10 minutes here daily. Sit quietly, breathe deeply, or write.

****Why this works**:*** Having a physical “safe zone” trains your brain to associate this spot with relaxation. Over time, just sitting there can trigger calmness.

****How to Live with Anxiety (Not Fight It)****

Anxiety may never fully disappear—and that's normal. The goal isn't to "fix" yourself but to build a kinder relationship with your anxiety. Here's how:

01. Practice Compassionate Self-Talk.

Replace self-criticism with kindness. For example:

- Instead of: *"Why am I so weak?!"*

- Try: *"This is hard right now. What do I need to feel safer?"*

Ask yourself: *"What does my anxiety need?"* Maybe it's rest, a walk, or talking to a friend.

02. Build Daily Rituals of Calm.

Small habits create a sense of stability:

- **10 minutes in nature**: Walk barefoot on grass, listen to leaves rustling.

- **Journaling**: Write 3 things you're grateful for each morning.

- **Tech-free tea time**: Sip herbal tea without distractions.

- **Gentle stretching**: Loosen tense muscles with slow movements.

03. Talk About It.

Shame grows in silence. Tell someone you trust:

"I've been feeling anxious lately. Just sharing this helps."

You don't need to explain or justify—just being heard can lighten the load.

04. Live *With* Anxiety, Not *After* It**

Don't wait for anxiety to vanish before enjoying life. Go to the party, take the trip, or try a new hobby—even if anxiety tags along. Over time, you'll learn that anxiety doesn't have to control your choices.

Final Thoughts

Anxiety is part of being human—a sign that your body cares deeply about your safety. By accepting it, grounding yourself in the present, and building small habits of care, you can turn down the volume of the "alarm" and reclaim your life. Progress isn't about being fearless; it's about moving forward even when fear is present. Remember: You are not your anxiety. It's a passing storm, and you are the sky—always vast, always whole, beneath it.

Tomorrow: Day 2 – The Science Behind Anxiety

We'll explore how your brain and nervous system respond to anxiety, and how to calm them with daily tools.

Day 2: The Science Behind Anxiety

Theme: Understand the brain to disarm fear.

Quote of the Day

"Your brain isn't trying to hurt you. It's trying to protect you — it just forgot how to relax." — Dr. Nicole Le Pera

---

Story 1: Leo and the Fire Alarm

Leo, a firefighter, knew danger better than most. Yet his most terrifying moments didn't happen during rescues — they happened in the quiet. While watching TV, his chest would tighten and his heart would race.

"I felt like I was dying," he admitted. Tests showed his heart was fine. His doctor explained, "Your brain is like a smoke detector going off with no fire." Leo realized he wasn't broken — he was overprotected by a brain stuck in 'survival mode.'

Story 2: A Child Called Panic

As a child, Fatima would panic during thunderstorms. She'd hide under the bed, convinced the sky was about to fall. As an adult, she still flinched at loud sounds and felt panic in crowded places. Her therapist explained that her amygdala — the brain's fear center — had been trained early on to react quickly.

Once Fatima understood her brain wasn't *against* her, she stopped feeling ashamed. She began speaking to her inner child with compassion.

The Brain and Anxiety: What's Really Going On?

The Key Players:

- **Amygdala** – The fear center. Triggers the fight/flight/freeze response.
- **Prefrontal Cortex** – The reasoning part. Helps assess actual threat.
- **Hippocampus** – Memory center. Connects current situations to past trauma.
- **Nervous System** – The body's communication highway between brain and organs.

When your brain **perceives** danger, it floods your body with:

- **Adrenaline** – Makes your heart race.
- **Cortisol** – Keeps you alert and wired.
- **Increased blood flow** – Prepares muscles to fight or flee.

Even when the threat isn't real, the brain reacts **as if it is**. That's anxiety: false alarm in a safe room.

Key Insight: It's Not You — It's Your Brain's Safety Programming

You're not weak, irrational, or broken. Your brain is working overtime to keep you alive. Understanding this takes the shame away — and gives you power back.

Daily Exercises and Solutions

1. The Hand Model of the Brain (Dr. Dan Siegel's Technique)

Make a fist with your thumb inside. Your **thumb** is the amygdala (emotions), and your **fingers** are the prefrontal cortex (logic).

When anxiety spikes, it's like your fingers "flip" — logic disconnects, and the amygdala takes over. Your goal? Breathe and reconnect the fingers. Bring logic back online.

Do this:

1. Clench and release your fist slowly 5x while breathing deeply.

2. As you breathe, say: *"I'm safe. My brain is learning to relax."*

---

2. Vagus Nerve Activation: Calm Your Body, Calm Your Brain

The vagus nerve is the body's **brake pedal**. Activate it to signal safety:

- **Cold water splash**: Run cool water over your face for 30 seconds.
- **Humming**: The vibrations stimulate the nerve and soothe you.
- **Deep belly breathing**: Inhale 4, hold 4, exhale 6.

Do this 3x today when feeling uneasy.

✅ 3. The "Real vs Imagined" Thought Test

Ask yourself:

- What am I afraid will happen?
- Is this happening *now*?
- Is there evidence it's true?
- What's a more helpful belief?

Example:

"I'll embarrass myself in the meeting." → "I've spoken before and was fine. It's okay to be nervous. I am prepared."

How to Live with an Anxious Brain

- **Talk to your brain like a worried child.** "I see you're scared, but we are okay. Let's breathe together."
- **Avoid "feeding the fear."** Reassure, don't obsess. Catch over-Googling or over-checking.
- **Do the opposite of anxiety.** If your brain tells you to hide, take one small action forward instead.
- **Give your brain recovery time.** Rest is not a reward — it's how your nervous system recalibrates.

Your Healing Journal Prompt

Complete the sentence:

"My anxiety is trying to protect me from ___, but I am learning to trust ___."

Then write one kind thing you will say to yourself next time anxiety strikes.

Affirmation of the Day

"My brain is learning that I am safe. I honor its protection, but I choose calm."

Tomorrow: Day 3 – Identifying Your Triggers

We'll dive into recognizing what sparks your anxiety, and how to defuse it before it overwhelms you.

Day 3: Identifying Your Triggers

Theme: Clarity precedes healing.

Quote of the Day

"Anxiety doesn't start in chaos — it starts in patterns. You can break the loop if you first notice the switch." — Dr. Caroline Leaf

---

Story: Sophia and the Silent Trigger

Sophia, a 42-year-old single mother, often experienced overwhelming panic in grocery stores. The fluorescent lights, the crowd, and the noise made her feel trapped. She'd abandon her cart and leave, heart pounding.

After journaling for a week, she discovered a pattern: these attacks only happened in large, crowded supermarkets. It reminded her of when she'd gotten lost as a child in a department store — terrified, unheard, and alone.

That memory had stayed buried in her nervous system, quietly shaping her adult reactions. Once she connected the dots, she worked with a therapist to gently reintroduce herself to these spaces using desensitization techniques. Eventually, she shopped without fear.

🔍 What Are Triggers?

A **trigger** is any stimulus — internal or external — that sets off an anxious response.

Triggers can be:

- **Situational:** Crowds, traffic, conflict, public speaking.
- **Sensory:** Loud noises, flashing lights, certain smells.
- **Emotional:** Feeling judged, unsupported, or unsafe.
- **Physical:** Fatigue, hunger, hormonal shifts.
- **Cognitive:** Specific thoughts or worries ("What if I fail?")

□ **Suggested Illustration:**

Diagram: "Common Trigger Categories"

- 5 icons or bubbles labeled: *Situational*, *Sensory*, *Emotional*, *Physical*, *Cognitive*

Key Insight: You Can't Heal What You Can't See

If anxiety feels random, it's terrifying. But when you discover the trigger, you gain power. You can prepare for it, reframe it, and eventually desensitize your response to it.

Daily Exercises and Solutions

1. Trigger Mapping Journal

Create two columns:

- **Trigger:** What caused the anxiety?
- **Reaction:** What happened in your body/mind?

Example:

Trigger	Reaction
Loud voice at work	Startled, tense shoulders, racing heart
Email from boss	Nausea, intrusive thoughts
Coffee on empty stomach	Shaky hands, restlessness

Do this every day for a week. Patterns will emerge.

---

2. Body Before Story Practice

Sometimes your body reacts *before* you know why. That's your subconscious at work.

When anxiety hits, pause and ask:

- What just happened?
- What did I see, hear, or think right before this?
- Where do I feel it in my body?
- Does this feeling remind me of something from the past?

This turns automatic fear into conscious awareness.

✅ 3. Trigger Tracker Card

Design a small pocket card (you can print or write it) with:

- Top 3 known triggers
- 1 grounding phrase
- 1 breath technique

Example Card:

- **Triggers:** Loud spaces, judgment, uncertainty
- **Phrase:** "This is a memory, not a danger."
- **Breath:** 4-4-6 (inhale 4, hold 4, exhale 6)

Keep it in your wallet or phone.

How to Live With Known Triggers

1. **Prepare, don't avoid.** Avoidance strengthens fear. Preparation empowers confidence.
2. **Use 'if/then' planning.**

"If I start to panic in the meeting, then I will excuse myself, take 5 breaths, and return when ready."

3. **Set boundaries.** It's okay to say no to people or situations that push you past your limit while you're healing.
4. **Share your map.** Tell a trusted person what triggers you and how they can help — you don't have to do this alone.

Story 2: Malik's Reclaiming Moment

Malik, 27, avoided driving after a minor car accident left him shaken. His chest would tighten on highways. His therapist helped him identify that the **sound of honking** was his main trigger. So Malik practiced listening to honking in controlled environments — watching driving videos with sound on, then sitting in a parked car, then short drives.

Step by step, his fear lost power. Triggers lose their grip when we approach them with gentleness, not avoidance.

Your Healing Journal Prompt

Write about a moment of recent anxiety. Then answer:

- What was happening right before it?
- What did you feel in your body?
- What thought ran through your mind?
- Was this a familiar feeling?

Close by writing:

"Now that I see it, I can change how I respond to it."

Affirmation of the Day

"I am becoming aware of what stirs my anxiety. I choose curiosity over fear."

Tomorrow: Day 4 – Breathing and Grounding Techniques

You'll learn how to instantly calm your nervous system using powerful breath work and grounding methods — your "emergency calm kit."

Day 4: Breathing and Grounding Techniques

Theme: Calm the body, and the mind will follow.

"Feelings are much like waves. We can't stop them from coming, but we can choose which ones to surf."

— Jonatan Mårtensson

Story: Kira's Public Speaking Terror

Kira was a talented architect, but any time she had to present her ideas in a meeting, her hands would tremble and her chest would tighten. One day, her therapist introduced her to a simple grounding breath: *Inhale for 4, hold for 4, exhale for 6.*

Before her next presentation, Kira excused herself to the restroom. She did the breath for two minutes. To her surprise, her mind slowed. Her heart rate calmed. For the first time in years, she got through a talk without spiraling. That breath became her anchor.

Why Breathing and Grounding Work

When you're anxious, your sympathetic nervous system activates — heart races, muscles tense, breath shortens.

To counter this, activate the **parasympathetic system** (your "rest and digest" mode). Breathing and grounding send signals of safety to the brain.

Daily Techniques

1. Box Breathing (Navy SEAL Technique)

- Inhale for 4 seconds
- Hold for 4 seconds
- Exhale for 4 seconds
- Hold for 4 seconds
- Repeat 4x

Use when: panic begins to rise, before stressful moments.

---

2. 5-4-3-2-1 Grounding Exercise

Name:

- 5 things you can see
- 4 things you can touch
- 3 things you can hear
- 2 things you can smell

- 1 thing you can taste

Use when: your thoughts spiral. It pulls you back to the present.

---

3. Tapping (EFT - Emotional Freedom Technique)

Gently tap 5–7 times on:

- Side of your hand
- Eyebrow
- Side of eye
- Under eye
- Collarbone
- Under your arm

Repeat affirmations like:

"Even though I feel anxious, I deeply love and accept myself."

Use when: anxiety feels stuck in the body.

Suggested Illustration:

A diagram showing:

- Nervous system (Sympathetic vs Parasympathetic)
- Box Breathing square
- Tapping point chart

Affirmation of the Day

"I breathe in calm. I breathe out fear."

Journal Prompt

Describe a recent anxiety moment. How did your body react? Try one technique today and record how you felt before and after.

Day 5: Challenging Negative Thought Patterns

*"You don't have to believe everything you think." – Unknown**

Anxiety often starts in the mind. A single thought can spiral into fear, panic, or sadness. But here's the good news: **you can stop anxiety where it begins—by changing how you think**. Today, we'll explore how to spot harmful thought patterns, challenge them, and replace them with kinder, truer ideas.

Understanding Cognitive Distortions

Your brain works like a muscle. Just as you might habitually slouch or bite your nails, your brain can fall into unhelpful thinking habits. These habits are called **cognitive distortions**—twisted or exaggerated thoughts that make situations feel worse than they are. They fuel anxiety by focusing on the negative, ignoring facts, or jumping to scary conclusions.

Let's break down common distortions with **real-life examples**:

1. **Catastrophizing**:

Expecting the worst possible outcome.

- *Thought:* “If I fail this test, I’ll never get into college, and my life will be ruined.”

- *Reality:* One test doesn’t define your future. Most problems have solutions.

2. **All-or-Nothing Thinking**:

Seeing things as perfect or terrible, with no middle ground.

- *Thought:* “If I’m not the best employee, I’m a total failure.”

- *Reality:* Success isn’t black-and-white. Progress matters more than perfection.

3. **Mind Reading**:

Assuming others think poorly of you without proof.

- *Thought:* “My friend didn’t text back. They hate me.”

- *Reality:* They might be busy, tired, or just forgot. You can't read minds.

4. **Overgeneralization**:

Using words like "always" or "never" based on one event.

- *Thought:* "I messed up my presentation. I'll *never* be good at public speaking."

- *Reality:* One mistake doesn't predict the future. Practice helps.

5. **Personalization**:

Blaming yourself for things you can't control.

- *Thought:* "My mom is upset. It's because I'm a bad daughter."

- *Reality:* Her mood could be about work, health, or something else entirely.

These thoughts often feel automatic, like a reflex. But with practice, you can **pause, question, and rewrite them**.

Story: Rewriting The Script

Meet **Tara**, a graphic designer who dreaded meetings with her boss. Every time her manager said, “Let’s chat,” Tara’s mind raced:

“She thinks I’m terrible at my job. I’ll get fired. I’ll lose my apartment. My life will fall apart.”

Tara’s anxiety was fueled by **catastrophizing**—assuming the worst. In therapy, she learned to:

1. **Write down the thought**: “I’m getting fired.”

2. **Name the distortion**: Catastrophizing.

3. **Challenge it**: *“Is there proof? No. My boss gives feedback often. Last month, she praised my work.”*

4. **Reframe it**: *“This is probably a routine check-in. Even if there’s criticism, I can learn from it.”*

Over time, Tara’s anxiety shrank. She still felt nervous before meetings, but she no longer let her thoughts control her.

The Reframing Technique: 4 Steps to Calmer Thoughts

Use this daily method to rewire your brain:

1. **Identify the Thought**

- *Ask:* “What’s the negative idea causing stress?”

- *Example:* “No one likes me.”

2. **Name the Distortion**

- *Ask:* “Which thinking habit is this?”

- *Example:* *Mind reading* (assuming others dislike you) + *Overgeneralization* (using “no one”).

3. **Challenge the Thought**

Ask:

- *“Is this 100% true? What’s the evidence?”*

- *For:* “Two people didn’t reply to my message.”

- *Against:* “Three friends invited me out last week.”

- *“What would I tell a friend who had this thought?”*

- *Example:* “You’re loved! People get busy—it’s not about you.”

4. **Reframe It**

Replace the thought with a balanced one:

- *Original:* “No one likes me.”

- *Reframed:* “Some people care about me, and others might just be busy. I’ll reach out to a friend to connect.”

Affirmations to Rewire Your Mind

Repeat these daily to build mental strength:

- **“My thoughts are not facts.”**

(Reminder: Just because you think it doesn’t make it true.)

- **“I challenge what doesn’t serve me.”**

(Ask: “Is this thought helpful or harmful?”)

- **“I deserve compassion—even from myself.”**

(Treat yourself like a friend.)

Daily Exercise: Thought Journal

Example Entry:

- **Anxious Thought:** “I’ll never find a job.”

- **Distortion:** Overgeneralization + Catastrophizing.

- **Evidence For:** “I’ve had three rejections this month.”

- **Evidence Against:** “I’ve gotten interviews. My skills are growing. Many people take time to find the right job.”

- **Reframed Thought:** “Job hunting is tough, but I’m making progress. Each interview teaches me something new.”

- **How I Feel Now:** Less hopeless, more determined.

Tip: Do this for 5 minutes daily. Track patterns—you’ll see progress over weeks!

Practical Remedy: The 5-Minute Evening Reframe

1. **Set a timer** for 5 minutes each night.

2. **Reflect**:

   - *"What anxious thoughts came up today?"*

     - *Example:* "I embarrassed myself at the party."

   - *"Which distortions were at play?"*

     - *Answer:* Personalization ("Everyone noticed my mistake!").

   - *"What's a kinder, truer thought?"*

     - *Reframe:* "Most people were focused on themselves. I had fun moments too!"

3. **Celebrate small wins**: "I caught my distortion today—that's growth!"

Final Thoughts

Challenging negative thoughts is like learning a new language—it takes time. You'll have days where old patterns creep back, and that's okay. What matters is **awareness** and **practice**. Every time you reframe a thought, you weaken anxiety's grip and build mental resilience.

Remember: **You are not your thoughts**. You're the person who can choose to let them go.

Tomorrow: Building a Self-Care Toolkit.

Day 6: Nutrition, Sleep, and Movement

"Your body hears everything your mind says. Feed it with love, rest, and movement." – Unknown

Your brain and body are not separate—what happens in one affects the other. Anxiety may feel like a purely mental struggle, but it often begins or worsens due to imbalances in how you eat, rest, and move. Today's focus is on aligning your physical health with your healing journey.

The Mind-Body Connection

Your body is the home of your nervous system—and your nervous system is the command center of anxiety. When your body is under stress from lack of sleep, poor diet, or inactivity, it sends signals to the brain that something is wrong, triggering anxious thoughts and sensations.

It works in reverse, too: when you nourish your body, calm your breath, and move with purpose, you send a message of safety to your brain. This reduces the "threat level" and restores inner balance.

Nutrition and Anxiety: Food as Fuel

What you eat directly impacts your mood, energy, and emotional regulation. Certain foods support your nervous system, while others can intensify anxiety symptoms like jitteriness, brain fog, and irritability.

Foods That Calm Anxiety:

- **Leafy greens (spinach, kale):** Rich in magnesium, which helps relax muscles and nerves.
- **Oats, brown rice, quinoa:** Slow-digesting carbs that stabilize blood sugar and serotonin.
- **Salmon, walnuts, chia seeds:** High in omega-3 fatty acids, which reduce inflammation and boost mood.
- **Fermented foods (yogurt, kefir, kimchi):** Support gut health—your "second brain."
- **Berries and citrus:** Packed with antioxidants that reduce oxidative stress.

Foods That May Trigger Anxiety:

- **Caffeine:** Can mimic symptoms of anxiety like rapid heartbeat and restlessness.
- **Sugar and refined carbs:** Cause blood sugar spikes and crashes, affecting mood and energy.
- **Alcohol:** Disrupts sleep and depletes key nutrients like B-vitamins and magnesium.
- **Processed foods:** Often high in additives that stress the nervous system.

Tip: Try keeping a simple food-mood journal this week. Track what you eat and how you feel an hour later. Patterns will emerge.

Sleep: Your Emotional Reset Button

Poor sleep doesn't just make you tired—it puts your body in a state of stress. Lack of deep sleep impacts the amygdala (the brain's fear center), making you more emotionally reactive and less resilient to stress.

Sleep Hygiene Tips for Anxiety Relief:

1. **Set a consistent sleep schedule:** Go to bed and wake up at the same time daily—even on weekends.
2. **Create a calming pre-sleep ritual:** Dim lights, turn off screens an hour before bed, and avoid stimulating activities.
3. **Limit caffeine and alcohol:** Especially in the afternoon and evening.
4. **Use your bed for sleep only:** No work or scrolling. This trains your brain to associate the bed with rest.
5. **Practice gratitude or gentle breathing:** Before sleep, write down three good things or do a body scan.

"Rest is not idleness, and to lie sometimes on the grass under trees... is by no means a waste of time." – John Lubbock

---

Movement: Medicine for the Mind

Exercise is one of the most underrated anxiety therapies available—and it's free. Moving your body releases endorphins (natural mood lifters), reduces cortisol (the stress hormone), and improves brain function.

Which Movements Help Most?

- **Walking in nature:** Lowers stress hormones and improves clarity.
- **Yoga or tai chi:** Combines physical movement with mindful breath and awareness.
- **Strength training:** Builds not just physical but mental resilience.
- **Dancing:** Reconnects you with joy and self-expression.

Story: Rohan's Turnaround

Rohan, a 32-year-old software developer, struggled with daily panic attacks and insomnia. Therapy helped him uncover deep-rooted fears, but real change came when he committed to 20 minutes of brisk walking every morning. After just two weeks, his energy improved, panic attacks lessened, and sleep became more restful. The movement had activated his body's natural anti-anxiety system.

Practical Exercise: Your Daily Wellness Plan

Use this 3-part self-care checklist every morning:

Nutrition:

☐ Did I eat a balanced breakfast?

☐ Am I drinking enough water today?

☐ Have I planned a nourishing lunch or dinner?

Sleep:

☐ Did I sleep at least 7–8 hours last night?

☐ What's one thing I can improve in my evening routine tonight?

Movement:

☐ Have I moved my body for at least 10 minutes today?

☐ Can I stretch or breathe mindfully this afternoon?

Affirmations for Physical Well-Being

- *"I honor my body with rest, fuel, and movement."*

- *"Each breath I take calms my nervous system."*
- *"I treat my body as a partner in healing."*
- *"I am building a healthy foundation for peace."*

Reflection Prompt

"What is one small change I can make today to better support my body in healing from anxiety?"

Maybe it's swapping coffee for herbal tea. Or adding a short walk after dinner. Start small—but start.

Healing Takes Holistic Care

Your mind needs your body to feel safe. You don't need to overhaul your diet overnight or become a fitness guru. Instead, think of your body like a garden: daily small acts of care—watering, weeding, nourishing—create a thriving, resilient ecosystem over time.

Tomorrow's Focus: Midweek Reset and Self-Reflection

You've reached Day 6—well done! Tomorrow, we'll pause to reflect on everything you've learned so far, identify your wins, and create space for integration before moving into the next phase of transformation.

Day 7: Reflect and Reset

"Almost everything will work again if you unplug it for a few minutes… including you." – Anne Lamott

Congratulations. You've completed the **first week** of your 21-day healing journey. That's no small accomplishment. You've shown up for yourself every single day—learning, practicing, and gently shifting the way you think, feel, and live. Today is not about doing more. It's about pausing to reflect, reset, and recharge.

Why is this important?

Because healing isn't linear. Some days you'll feel strong and empowered. Others, you'll feel like you've taken a few steps back. That's not failure—it's *normal*. Today, we acknowledge the progress you've made and give your mind and body the space to absorb the work you've done so far.

Why Reflection Matters

In a world obsessed with productivity, we often overlook rest. But in psychology and personal growth, rest and reflection are essential. When you reflect, you:

- Recognize patterns and progress.
- Integrate new learning.
- Celebrate small victories.
- Realign your intentions with compassion.

Think of today as a gentle exhale—a moment to stop climbing and look at how far you've already come.

Week One Recap: The Foundations of Healing

Let's look back at what you've covered so far:

Day 1: Facing the Truth About Anxiety

You explored what anxiety really is and took an honest inventory of how it shows up in your life.

Day 2: The Science Behind Anxiety

You learned how your brain, body, and nervous system interact to produce anxious thoughts and feelings.

Day 3: Identifying Your Triggers

You began recognizing what sparks your anxiety—and how to track it with awareness rather than judgment.

Day 4: Breathing and Grounding Techniques

You practiced calming your nervous system through breath and body awareness.

Day 5: Challenging Negative Thought Patterns

You uncovered cognitive distortions and started reframing anxiety-producing thoughts.

Day 6: Nutrition, Sleep, and Movement

You learned how caring for your body supports emotional resilience and nervous system balance.

That’s a lot of progress in just one week. Take a moment to feel that.

Mini Self-Assessment: How Are You Feeling Now?

Use the checklist below to evaluate your current state compared to Day 1.

Emotionally:
☐ More aware of my feelings
☐ Less overwhelmed by anxious thoughts
☐ Better able to pause and breathe

Physically:
☐ Sleeping more restfully

☐ Eating more mindfully
☐ Incorporating movement into my day

Mentally:

☐ Catching negative thoughts more easily
☐ Using reframing techniques
☐ Journaling or reflecting regularly

Which areas feel strongest right now? Which still feel shaky? No judgment—just observation.

Reflection Exercise: Then vs. Now

Take a few moments to journal your answers:

1. **What have I learned about my anxiety this week?**

   ---

2. **Which practice or insight has helped me the most so far?**

   ---

3. **What surprised me about myself?**

   ---

4. **How do I want to feel by Day 21?**

This is your story. Own it with honesty and hope.

Story: A Step Forward Is Still Forward

Emily, a mother of two in her 40s, started her anxiety healing journey with skepticism. "I've tried everything," she told herself. "Nothing works for me." But by Day 7 of a structured plan like yours, she noticed something small but meaningful—when her child had a meltdown, she didn't spiral. She paused, breathed, and responded calmly.

"I still felt anxious," she said, "but I wasn't *controlled* by it. And that felt like freedom."

Remember: the goal isn't to erase anxiety. It's to learn how to live with it—peacefully and powerfully.

Affirmations for Reflection and Compassion

- *"I honor the progress I've made."*
- *"Every breath is a new beginning."*
- *"I am learning to care for myself in new ways."*

- *"I release the need to be perfect. Progress is enough."*
- *"Healing happens in layers. I trust the process."*

Repeat these today—write them in your journal or speak them aloud as you walk, sit quietly, or prepare for sleep.

Gentle Reset: Today's Suggestions

Here are five simple ways to reset and recharge:

1. **Unplug:** Spend one hour away from your phone or devices. Let your brain breathe.
2. **Take a Nature Walk:** No agenda. Just walk, observe, and let the world ground you.
3. **Create Space:** Clean or organize a small area—your desk, a drawer, or your digital files. Outer clarity supports inner calm.
4. **Hydrate and Nourish:** Drink extra water. Eat slowly. Taste your food.
5. **Rest Without Guilt:** Take a nap, meditate, or simply *do nothing* for 15 minutes.

You don't always need to "do" more to heal. Sometimes, the most powerful thing you can do is pause.

Reflection Prompt

"What does rest mean to me—and how can I give myself permission to embrace it today?"

Write your answer. Breathe into it. Let it guide how you move through your day.

Closing Words

This is your healing journey—and no one else's. You're not behind. You're not failing. You're learning, showing up, and growing in ways you may not fully see yet.

Tomorrow, you'll begin **Week 2: Tools for Transformation**—where we go deeper into mindfulness, emotional processing, boundaries, and self-empowerment.

But today? Celebrate your courage. Celebrate your commitment.

Coming Up: Day 8 — Mindfulness and Presence

You've built your foundation. Now, let's explore how living in the present moment—free from past regrets or future worries—can bring clarity and calm to even your most anxious days.

Until then… rest well. You're doing beautifully.

Part II:

Tools for Transformation (Days 8-14) — Rewiring and Rebuilding

Day 8: Mindfulness and Presence

"Mindfulness is the key to a happy and peaceful life in the present moment." – Thich Nhat Hanh

Welcome to **Week Two: Tools for Transformation**. You've laid the foundation by understanding anxiety, identifying your triggers, and beginning to care for your body and mind. Now it's time to *rewire* how you respond to life's moments. And we begin with one of the most powerful tools of all—**mindfulness**.

What Is Mindfulness?

Mindfulness means paying attention, on purpose, to the present moment—**without judgment**. It sounds simple, yet it's life-changing. When you become mindful, you stop living on autopilot. You stop spiraling into worries about the future or regrets about the past.

Instead, you learn to *be here*. With your breath. With your body. With what is.

Mindfulness doesn't "fix" anxiety. Instead, it helps you **respond** to it differently. It creates space between you and your thoughts. And in that space, healing begins.

The Anxiety–Mindfulness Connection

Anxiety thrives in the *what-ifs* of tomorrow.

"What if I fail?"
"What if something bad happens?"
"What if I lose control?"

Mindfulness grounds you in *what is*—this breath, this moment, this now.

Research has shown that regular mindfulness practice:

- Lowers cortisol levels (your body's stress hormone)
- Improves focus and emotional regulation
- Strengthens areas of the brain related to calm, decision-making, and empathy

Even a few minutes a day can begin to reshape how your brain responds to stress.

Guided Mindfulness Practice: 5 Minutes to Peace

Find a quiet place. Sit comfortably. Close your eyes or soften your gaze.

1. **Breathe:** Inhale slowly through your nose for 4 seconds. Hold for 2 seconds. Exhale gently through your mouth for 6 seconds.
2. **Anchor:** Bring your attention to your breath. Feel it in your nostrils, chest, or belly.
3. **Notice:** Thoughts will come. That's okay. Don't fight them. Just notice: *"There's a thought."* Then gently bring your attention back to the breath.
4. **Repeat:** Do this for 5 minutes. If your mind wanders 100 times, bring it back 101. That *is* the practice.

Try this every morning or evening. Over time, it becomes a trusted refuge.

Story: Raj's Morning Pause

Raj was a high-achieving engineer who struggled with panic attacks. His mornings were chaotic—emails, news, coffee, racing thoughts. He began each day anxious and reactive. Then, he started a 10-minute mindfulness routine. Just breathing and observing.

After two weeks, he noticed a shift. He was still busy—but calmer. His anxiety hadn't vanished, but he no longer felt *swallowed* by it.

"That small pause in the morning became the strongest part of my day," he said. "It gave me my power back."

Daily Mindfulness in Action

Mindfulness isn't just about meditation. It's about how you live each moment.

Here's how to bring it into daily life:

- **Mindful Eating:** Take one meal a day to eat slowly, without distractions. Chew fully. Taste. Notice textures.
- **Mindful Walking:** Leave your phone behind. Feel your feet touch the ground. Notice sounds, colors, smells.
- **Mindful Listening:** The next time someone speaks, just listen. Don't plan your response. Just be present.
- **Mindful Waiting:** Waiting in line or on hold? Breathe. Observe your surroundings. Practice patience with presence.

Affirmations for Mindful Presence

- *"I am here, in this moment."*
- *"My breath is my anchor to peace."*
- *"I release the need to control the future."*
- *"Each moment is a new beginning."*

Say these silently during your mindfulness practice or write them on a sticky note near your bed or workspace.

Reflection Prompt

"Where in my day do I most often lose presence—and how can I create space to return to it?"

Maybe it's during your commute, meetings, or parenting. Awareness is the first step. Even 30 seconds of presence is powerful.

Common Myths About Mindfulness

Let's clear up a few misconceptions:

- **"I have to clear my mind."**
No. Your mind will think. Your job is to *observe*, not eliminate thoughts.
- **"I don't have time."**
Even 2 minutes counts. Mindfulness is about *quality*, not quantity.
- If you notice your mind wandering, *you're doing it right.* That's the practice.

Be patient. This is a skill. And like all skills, it strengthens with repetition.

Mini Practice: STOP Method

A quick mindfulness technique you can use anytime anxiety strikes:

S – Stop what you're doing.
T – Take a breath.
O – Observe: What am I feeling? What's happening in my body?
P – Proceed with intention.

Try this today during a stressful moment—whether you're in traffic, at work, or caught in overthinking.

Mindfulness as a Lifestyle

Eventually, mindfulness becomes less of a "thing you do" and more of a *way you are*. You start:

- Responding instead of reacting.
- Pausing before spiraling.
- Feeling more peace in ordinary moments.

It doesn't happen overnight. But it begins today—with this breath.

Tomorrow's Focus: Emotional Acceptance

Now that you're learning to be present, tomorrow we'll explore the power of *feeling* emotions without judgment or fear. You'll learn how to embrace anxiety—not as an enemy, but as a messenger.

You are not behind. You are right on time. Keep going.

Day 9: Emotional Acceptance

"What you resist, persists. What you feel, you can heal." – Carl Jung

You've practiced mindfulness and learned how to be present. Today, we go one step deeper—**accepting** what you feel rather than fighting it.

For most people with anxiety, emotions like fear, sadness, anger, or overwhelm feel *unwelcome.* We push them away, suppress them, or distract ourselves. But the truth is: emotions don't disappear when ignored. They grow louder, trying to get your attention.

Emotional acceptance is the brave act of saying, *"It's okay to feel this."* Even when it's uncomfortable. Even when it's messy.

Why Emotional Avoidance Fuels Anxiety

When you avoid emotions, you unintentionally teach your brain that feelings are dangerous. This triggers the anxiety cycle:

1. You feel a difficult emotion (e.g., fear).
2. You try to suppress or avoid it.
3. Your body senses danger, activating anxiety.
4. Anxiety makes the emotion feel even worse.

By learning to *sit with emotions*, you break this cycle.

What Is Emotional Acceptance?

Emotional acceptance means:

- Allowing emotions to be there without judgment.
- Recognizing that all emotions are valid and temporary.
- Creating space to feel, process, and move forward.

It doesn't mean *liking* the emotion. It simply means acknowledging its presence—like letting a storm pass without trying to stop the rain.

The RAIN Method

A powerful tool for emotional acceptance is the **RAIN** method, developed by meditation teacher Tara Brach. It's simple, effective, and can be done anytime.

R — Recognize

Notice what you're feeling. *"I'm feeling anxious. I'm feeling sad. I'm feeling tight in my chest."*

A — Allow

Let the feeling be there without trying to fix it. *"It's okay to feel this way right now."*

I — Investigate

Gently explore what's going on. *"Why might I be feeling this? What does this emotion need from me?"*

N — Nurture

Offer yourself compassion. *"I'm doing the best I can. I'm safe. I'm allowed to feel this."*

Use RAIN the next time anxiety arises. Write each step in a journal or walk yourself through it silently.

Story: Jasmine and the Wall of Emotion

Jasmine always described herself as "too emotional." As a child, she was told to "stop crying" and "be strong." So she learned to push everything down.

In adulthood, her anxiety felt uncontrollable—especially in moments of grief, anger, or disappointment. Through therapy, she learned emotional acceptance. Instead of bottling her feelings, she started naming them, breathing with them, and allowing herself to *feel* without shame.

"It was scary at first," she said, "but eventually, those emotions stopped owning me. They became visitors, not monsters."

The Anatomy of an Emotion

Most emotions, if allowed, last **90 seconds** in the body. That's it.

What makes them last longer is the **story** we attach to them:

- "I shouldn't feel this way."
- "What's wrong with me?"
- "This feeling will never go away."

When you let the emotion move through you—like a wave—it peaks and passes. You come out the other side stronger.

Practical Exercise: The Emotional Body Scan

Find a quiet space. Sit or lie down.

1. Close your eyes and breathe deeply.
2. Bring awareness to your body from head to toe.
3. Where are you holding tension? Tight jaw? Clenched fists? Racing heart?
4. Name the emotion associated with each sensation.

Example: "Tight chest = fear." "Heavy shoulders = worry."

5. Breathe into that space. Say silently: *"I see you. It's okay to feel this."*

Repeat as often as needed throughout the day.

Affirmations for Emotional Acceptance

- *"I am allowed to feel all of my emotions."*
- *"I honor my feelings without judgment."*
- *"This emotion is temporary."*
- *"I create space for healing by being present with myself."*

Say these when you're feeling overwhelmed. They serve as reminders that emotions are not enemies—they are signals.

Reflection Prompt

"What emotion do I avoid the most—and what would happen if I gave it permission to be seen?"

Journal your honest answer. Even naming the emotion you resist can begin to release its grip.

Releasing Resistance

Here are a few signs that you're resisting emotion:

- Constant busyness or distraction
- Feeling numb or detached
- Irritability without clear cause
- Anxiety that feels "random" or unexplained

To soften this resistance, try:

- Saying "yes" internally when an emotion rises
- Placing a hand on your heart and offering self-kindness
- Reminding yourself: *"I can survive this feeling."*

Emotional acceptance is *not* weakness. It's courage in its truest form.

What If the Emotion Feels Too Big?

If an emotion feels overwhelming:

- Breathe slowly and deeply
- Ground yourself with touch (hold an object, press your feet into the floor)
- Reach out to a friend, therapist, or support line
- Move your body—dance, walk, stretch

Sometimes emotions need movement, not just stillness.

You're Rewriting Old Patterns

If you've spent years suppressing emotions, this work may feel unfamiliar—even uncomfortable. That's okay.

Every time you sit with a feeling instead of pushing it away, you're:

- Building emotional resilience
- Teaching your nervous system that you are safe
- Healing wounds that began long ago

You're not just managing anxiety—you're transforming your relationship with yourself.

Tomorrow's Focus: Journaling for Clarity

Tomorrow, we'll dive into the powerful practice of **journaling**—a tool for clearing mental clutter, tracking anxiety patterns, and deepening emotional self-awareness.

Until then, take a deep breath. You're doing deep work. And it matters.

Day 10: Journaling for Clarity

"Journal writing is a voyage to the interior." – Christina Baldwin

Anxiety lives in the mind like clutter in a crowded room—thoughts scattered, fears piled high, feelings buried beneath layers of confusion. Today's healing tool is your personal flashlight: **journaling**.

Writing isn't just an outlet. It's a powerful form of self-therapy. It helps you name what's swirling in your mind, connect the dots, and access clarity where chaos once lived.

Why Journaling Helps Anxiety

An anxious brain is often filled with "what ifs," spirals, and unresolved fears. Journaling offers three major benefits:

1. **It Slows the Mind** – Writing by hand naturally decelerates your thoughts.
2. **It Externalizes Worries** – Instead of holding everything in, you let it out.
3. **It Creates Insight** – You begin to see patterns, triggers, and solutions.

Your journal becomes a mirror—not to criticize, but to understand.

Types of Journaling That Heal

You don't need to be a writer or use perfect grammar. What matters is **honesty**. Here are a few anxiety-relieving journaling styles:

1. Freewriting (Brain Dump)

Set a timer for 10–15 minutes. Write nonstop. Don't censor yourself. Don't edit. Let your thoughts pour out, even if they don't make sense.
Prompt: "What's really on my mind right now?"

2. Trigger Tracker

After an anxious moment, write:

- What happened?
- What did I feel?
- What thought triggered it?
- How did I react?
- What would I like to do differently next time?

This builds emotional intelligence and self-awareness.

3. Gratitude Journaling

Anxiety often focuses on lack or fear. Gratitude refocuses the brain on abundance and safety. *Prompt:* "Today I'm thankful for…"

4. Dialogue Journaling

Write a conversation between you and your anxiety. Give your anxiety a voice, and respond as your wiser self. *Prompt:* "Dear Anxiety, why are you here today?"

Story: Aaron's 10-Minute Breakthrough

Aaron was a college student who'd been struggling with anxiety for years. He kept most of it to himself, believing that writing wasn't "his thing."

One day, during a panic episode, he tried freewriting for the first time. He wrote everything he felt—fear, shame, pressure. By the time he looked up, tears were falling. He'd uncovered something important: he wasn't afraid of failure. He was afraid of *disappointing others*.

That insight changed everything. He began journaling every morning for 10 minutes. It became his sacred space to breathe and reflect. In time, he stopped seeing journaling as a chore—and started seeing it as healing.

Daily Anxiety Journal Template

If you're unsure where to start, use this simple format each day:

1. **Today I feel…** (Name your emotion without judgment)
2. **What triggered me today?** (Write the situation or thought)
3. **What did I tell myself?** (Identify the inner dialogue)
4. **Is it true?** (Challenge distorted thinking)
5. **What can I choose instead?** (Reframe with a more supportive truth)
6. **Something I'm proud of today:** (Celebrate even the small wins)
7. **One thing I'm grateful for:** (Shift into appreciation)

This takes 5–10 minutes and offers consistent emotional clarity.

Affirmations for Clarity and Self-Reflection

- *"I give myself permission to express what I feel."*
- *"My thoughts do not define me. They are just thoughts."*
- *"I write my way to healing."*

- *"I am safe in my inner world."*

Repeat one of these before journaling, like a ritual that opens your heart and quiets your fear.

Reflection Prompt for Today

"If my anxiety could speak, what would it say? What would I say back?"

Write this as a letter, dialogue, or list. Let your inner self respond with compassion—not fear.

Creating a Journaling Habit

To make journaling effective, consistency is key. Here's how to build your practice:

- **Choose a set time** (morning reflection or nighttime release)
- **Keep your journal visible** (on your pillow, desk, or in your bag)
- **Create a calming ritual** (light a candle, play soft music, take deep breaths)
- **Start small** (even 5 minutes counts)

You’re not writing a masterpiece—you’re witnessing your truth.

What If I Don’t Know What to Write?

If your mind goes blank, try:

- “Right now, I feel…”
- “The last time I felt peaceful was…”
- “I want to understand why…”
- “One thing I’m scared to admit is…”

There are no wrong answers. Your journal is your judgment-free zone.

How Journaling Shifts the Brain

Research shows that expressive writing:

- Reduces cortisol (stress hormone)
- Strengthens cognitive processing
- Increases emotional regulation
- Improves sleep and focus

In short: journaling doesn’t just *feel* good—it’s scientifically healing.

Your Journal as a Timeline of Growth

One of the most beautiful things about journaling is looking back.

Weeks or months from now, you'll flip through pages and realize:

- "Wow, I don't think like that anymore."
- "I survived that hard moment."
- "I've come so far."

Your past entries become proof of your resilience.

Tomorrow's Focus: Setting Boundaries

Tomorrow, we'll explore the healing power of saying *no*—how boundaries create emotional safety, reduce anxiety, and honor your energy.

Until then, keep your pen close and your heart open. You are learning to hear yourself clearly—and that is a radical act of self-love.

Day 11: Setting Boundaries

"Daring to set boundaries is about having the courage to love ourselves, even when we risk disappointing others."* – *Brené Brown

One of the most powerful tools in your anxiety healing journey is often overlooked: **boundaries**.

When your energy is constantly drained, when you say "yes" but mean "no," when you tolerate toxic patterns just to keep the peace—your anxiety has no room to rest.

Today, we reclaim your right to peace by exploring healthy emotional boundaries.

What Are Boundaries, Really?

Boundaries are the invisible lines that define where *you* end and *others* begin. They help protect your time, energy, emotions, and mental space.

There are many types:

- **Physical boundaries:** Personal space, touch
- **Emotional boundaries:** Not absorbing others' emotions
- **Mental boundaries:** Protecting your thoughts, beliefs

- **Time boundaries:** Managing your availability
- **Energetic boundaries:** Saying no to people or tasks that leave you depleted

Strong boundaries are not walls. They are bridges to healthier relationships—with others *and* yourself.

Why Weak Boundaries Trigger Anxiety

If you struggle with people-pleasing, guilt, or overcommitment, you might find it hard to say "no." But when you constantly override your own needs, anxiety builds.

Here's why:

- You feel resentful but say nothing.
- You suppress your truth to avoid conflict.
- You live for others' approval and feel disconnected from your authentic self.

Every time you abandon your own needs, your nervous system feels unsafe. Boundaries restore that safety.

Signs You Need Stronger Boundaries

- You feel anxious when asked for favors.

- You dread certain interactions but can't avoid them.
- You say "yes" and instantly regret it.
- You feel guilty for resting or taking space.
- You often think, *"I can't disappoint them."*

If any of these sound familiar, it's time to realign.

Story: Maya and the Courage to Say No

Maya worked in a high-pressure job and was known as "the dependable one." She said yes to every project, worked weekends, and rarely took time off.

Behind closed doors, she was exhausted, anxious, and on the verge of burnout.

One day, after yet another sleepless night, she decided to say "no" to a last-minute assignment. Her voice trembled. Her heart raced.

To her surprise, the world didn't fall apart. Her manager respected her honesty. That moment was her turning point.

Maya began saying yes only when she meant it. Her anxiety decreased. Her self-respect grew.

Practical Tool: The Boundary Scripts

Here are some simple phrases you can practice and use:

- *"I'm not available for that right now."*
- *"Thank you for thinking of me, but I'll have to pass."*
- *"That doesn't work for me."*
- *"I need some time to think about it."*
- *"I'm not comfortable discussing this."*

These statements are kind, clear, and firm. They protect your peace without inviting guilt.

How to Set Boundaries Without Guilt

Guilt often creeps in after setting a boundary, especially if you're used to self-sacrifice. But remember:

- You are not responsible for others' reactions.
- You don't need to over-explain or justify.
- Saying "no" to others is often saying "yes" to yourself.

Repeat this mantra:

"My needs matter just as much as anyone else's."

Reflection Prompt

"Where in my life am I saying yes out of fear, guilt, or obligation?"

Write honestly. Then, ask yourself:

- What would it feel like to say no?
- What would I gain by honoring my truth?

Let this awareness guide your next steps.

Boundary Visualization Exercise

1. Close your eyes. Take a deep breath.
2. Imagine a golden circle of light around you.
3. Inside this circle is your peace, energy, and emotional space.
4. Now imagine someone or something crossing that circle. How does it feel?
5. Visualize gently placing your hands up and saying, *"Not today. I honor myself."*

This practice helps you embody the feeling of inner safety and protection.

Affirmations for Boundaries

- *"It is safe to honor my needs."*
- *"I release the need to please everyone."*
- *"My peace is more important than their approval."*
- *"I choose relationships that nourish, not drain, me."*

Use these daily, especially when preparing to set or reinforce a boundary.

Healing Through Boundaries

When you set boundaries:

- Anxiety decreases because you stop abandoning yourself.
- Your relationships improve because they're built on mutual respect.
- You feel empowered, not overwhelmed.

This isn't about being selfish—it's about being **self-aware**.

Mini-Challenge: Set One Small Boundary Today

Choose one low-stakes boundary to practice today:

- Say no to a request.

- Take a full lunch break without interruptions.
- Turn your phone on "Do Not Disturb."
- Delay responding to messages until *you* feel ready.

Notice how your body responds. Do you feel lighter? Empowered? Nervous? All of these are normal. You're retraining your system for emotional safety.

Remember This

- Boundaries are not punishments—they are self-respect in action.
- You can be kind *and* firm.
- Every "no" you say creates space for a more intentional "yes."

You deserve to feel safe in your body, your mind, and your relationships. Boundaries are how you build that safety—one decision at a time.

Tomorrow's Focus: Reclaiming Control

Anxiety often comes from feeling powerless. In Day 12, we'll learn how to take back control through visualization, goal-setting, and celebrating small wins.

Until then, celebrate this: today, you protected your peace. That's healing in motion.

Day 12: Reclaiming Control

"You may not control all the events that happen to you, but you can decide not to be reduced by them." – Maya Angelou

Anxiety often feels like you're trapped in a whirlwind—your thoughts racing, your emotions pulling you in every direction, and your sense of power slipping away.

But today, we flip the narrative.

Today, you begin to **reclaim control**.

Not over everything. Not over others. But over the one thing you *can* influence: **your response**.

Why Control Matters

Loss of control is one of the biggest contributors to anxiety. When we feel like life is happening *to* us, we freeze, panic, or give up.

Reclaiming control doesn't mean micromanaging everything. It means anchoring yourself to what you can do—**right here, right now**.

This shift is empowering. It tells your brain, "I'm not helpless. I can respond. I have choices."

The Circle of Control Exercise

Draw two circles.

- The inner circle is your **Circle of Control** – things you can influence (your habits, your breath, your words, your mindset).
- The outer circle is your **Circle of Concern** – things you worry about but can't change directly (others' opinions, world events, the past).

Now ask yourself:

"Am I spending my energy in my Circle of Control or my Circle of Concern?"

When anxiety spikes, it often means you're stuck in the outer circle. Today's goal is to return to the center.

Story: Liam's Shift to Power

Liam had been battling anxiety for years. He obsessed over what people thought of him, replayed awkward moments, and feared the worst in every situation.

In therapy, he learned about the Circle of Control. He realized he was giving *all* his energy to things outside of himself.

So he started small. He committed to a morning routine. He journaled his thoughts daily. He turned off notifications when he felt overwhelmed.

Each action wasn't huge—but collectively, they helped Liam feel grounded, capable, and clear. His anxiety lessened—not because the world changed, but because he did.

Small Wins = Big Momentum

When anxiety is strong, doing *anything* can feel impossible. That's why we focus on **small wins**.

A small win might be:

- Making your bed.
- Drinking water first thing.
- Taking five deep breaths.
- Saying no to something draining.
- Speaking up for yourself.

Each small win is a message to your brain: *"I'm capable. I'm moving forward."*

Celebrate these! Write them down. Let them fuel your momentum.

The Power of Visualization

Your brain doesn't always distinguish between imagined and real experiences. That's why **visualization** is such a powerful tool for anxiety.

Try This:

1. Close your eyes.
2. Picture a version of you who feels calm, grounded, and in control.
3. What are they doing? What do they say? How do they move?
4. Imagine stepping into their shoes. Let their energy become yours.

Do this for 2–3 minutes daily. Over time, this vision becomes your reality.

Daily Control Ritual

Each morning, ask yourself:

- *"What is one thing I can control today that supports my peace?"*
- *"What is one small win I want to create today?"*

Then take action. Let the act of choosing be your anchor.

Affirmations to Reclaim Control

- *"I choose to focus on what I can control."*
- *"I am not powerless—I have options."*
- *"Even small actions create powerful change."*
- *"My peace is in my choices, not my circumstances."*

Say these aloud, write them in your journal, or post them where you'll see them often.

Reframing the Anxious Mind

An anxious mind often asks, *"What if something goes wrong?"*

A controlled, empowered mind asks:

"What if I handle it better than I ever imagined?"

Reframing is not denying fear—it's choosing hope. And every time you choose hope, you take back a little more control.

Reflection Prompt

"Where in my life am I giving away my power? What's one small step I can take to reclaim it today?"

Write without censoring. Be honest. Even naming where you feel powerless is a step toward reclaiming your strength.

Grounding Practice: The Control Shift

Here's a quick 5-minute grounding exercise for anxious moments:

1. **Pause.** Take a deep breath.
2. **Acknowledge.** Say, "I'm feeling anxious—and that's okay."
3. **Ask.** "What can I control right now?" (Even if it's just your breath)
4. **Act.** Take one small action—stretch, hydrate, journal, step outside.
5. **Affirm.** "I did something for myself. I'm in motion."

This practice tells your nervous system, *"We're not stuck. We're safe."*

Bonus Tip: Create a Control List

On one page of your journal, create two columns:

- **What I Can Control**
- **What I Release**

Revisit this whenever you feel overwhelmed. It helps you refocus and breathe easier.

You Are Not Helpless

Yes, anxiety is real. It can be heavy and confusing. But every single day, you have tools, choices, and moments that *are* within your reach.

When you choose your response, when you take that first step, when you celebrate even the tiniest win—you're healing.

You're coming back to yourself.

Tomorrow's Focus: Affirmations and Self-Talk

Next, we'll dive deep into the language you speak to yourself—how your inner voice can either fuel anxiety or empower your peace. It's time to rewire your self-talk and speak with love, not fear.

Until then, take one small action today—and reclaim your power.

Day 13: Affirmations and Self-Talk

"Be careful how you talk to yourself. You're always listening." – Unknown

The voice you hear the most isn't from a loved one, a critic, or a friend—it's your **own voice**.

Every thought you think, every belief you reinforce, every word you say to yourself has power. That voice can either **soothe your anxiety** or **amplify it**.

Today, we explore one of the most transformative tools in emotional healing: **affirmations and self-talk**.

What Is Self-Talk?

Self-talk is your internal dialogue—what you say to yourself silently throughout the day. It shapes your perception of who you are, what you're capable of, and how you experience the world.

Anxiety often stems from negative, catastrophic, or self-defeating self-talk:

- *"I can't handle this."*
- *"Something bad is going to happen."*
- *"I'm not good enough."*

When repeated, these thoughts become **mental grooves**—deep patterns in the brain. But here's the beautiful truth: **you can change the script.**

Understanding Affirmations

Affirmations are **positive, present-tense statements** designed to retrain your brain to think more constructively.

When used consistently, affirmations:

- Create new neural pathways
- Increase emotional resilience
- Reduce anxiety and stress
- Boost confidence and self-worth

But they must be **meaningful**, **believable**, and **consistent**.

Story: Sarah's Silent Transformation

Sarah had a loud inner critic. She called herself "weak" whenever she felt anxious and often replayed her mistakes.

One day, she decided to challenge that voice. She wrote down one affirmation: *"I am doing my best, and that's enough."*

At first, it felt fake. But she stuck with it. Every morning, she said it out loud. Every time she spiraled, she repeated it. Slowly, her anxiety softened.

Eventually, she added more affirmations, built a ritual around them, and noticed a radical shift—not just in her thoughts, but in her life.

Your words matter. Your voice matters. Use it to lift yourself, not tear yourself down.

Affirmations for Anxiety Healing

Here are powerful affirmations you can begin using today:

- *"I am safe in this moment."*
- *"I am capable of handling what comes my way."*
- *"I choose peace over fear."*
- *"I am not my thoughts—I am the awareness behind them."*
- *"I release what I cannot control."*
- *"It's okay to feel anxious; I am still worthy of love and compassion."*

Choose 2–3 that resonate. Write them. Say them out loud. Breathe them in.

Crafting Your Own Affirmations

To create personalized affirmations, follow this simple formula:

1. **Use present tense** (e.g., *"I am..."* not *"I will..."*)
2. **Keep it positive** (Focus on what you want, not what you fear)
3. **Keep it specific** (Tailor it to your emotional needs)
4. **Make it believable** (You must be able to grow into it)

Example:
Instead of "I am never anxious" (unrealistic), try: *"I am learning to stay calm even in difficult moments."*

Morning and Evening Affirmation Routine

Morning (5 minutes)

- Find a quiet space.
- Stand in front of a mirror.
- Say 3 affirmations while looking into your eyes.
- Smile gently after each one.
- Take a deep breath and carry that energy with you.

Evening (5 minutes)

- Before bed, place a hand on your heart.
- Whisper affirmations softly.
- Imagine the words soaking into your soul.
- Reflect on one moment in the day where you honored your growth.

Let this practice become sacred.

How Affirmations Rewire the Brain

Neuroscience shows that **repeated thoughts create and strengthen neural connections**. With consistent affirmation practice:

- The negative voice loses its power.
- Your default reaction becomes calmer and more grounded.
- You begin to believe in your own inner strength.

This is **mental fitness**—training your brain toward peace.

Combating the Inner Critic

Everyone has an inner critic. But here's a powerful technique to disarm it:

The 3-Step Self-Talk Reframe:

1. **Catch it** – Notice when the negative thought appears.
2. **Challenge it** – Ask, *"Is this absolutely true?"*
3. **Change it** – Replace it with a kinder truth.

Example:
Negative thought: *"I'm so weak for feeling anxious."*
Reframe: *"I'm strong for showing up while feeling anxious."*

Repeat the new truth. Let it become your new reality.

Affirmations in Anxious Moments

When anxiety hits suddenly, affirmations can act as emotional CPR.

Try this:

- Place one hand on your chest, the other on your belly.
- Breathe deeply.
- Say aloud:

"This feeling will pass."
"I am safe."
"I choose calm."

Let the words slow your heart. Let them anchor you in the now.

Reflection Prompt

"What do I often say to myself that fuels my anxiety? What could I say instead that empowers me?"

Take your time with this one. Awareness is the first step to change. Your voice deserves compassion—especially when you're struggling.

Sticky Note Power

Here's a fun, simple practice:
Write your top 3 affirmations on sticky notes. Place them:

- On your mirror
- Beside your bed
- On your laptop or fridge

Let these notes become soft reminders throughout your day. They whisper: *"You've got this."*

You Deserve a Kind Voice

There's enough noise in the world trying to bring you down.

Make your inner voice the one place you always feel safe, supported, and seen.

You don't need to be perfect. You just need to be present—and kind to yourself.

Tomorrow's Focus: Reflect and Reset

Tomorrow marks the end of Week Two. We'll pause, reflect on your incredible progress, and reset for the final stretch of your 21-day journey.

Until then, speak gently to yourself.

You're listening.

Day 14: Reflect and Reset

"Sometimes the most productive thing you can do is pause and reflect." – Unknown

You've just completed two full weeks of inner work, self-discovery, and emotional healing.

Take a moment right now… and **breathe.**

Seriously. Stop reading for a second.

Breathe in.

Hold it.

Exhale slowly.

Now think back over the last 13 days. You've learned how to identify your anxiety, ground yourself in the moment, reshape your thoughts, care for your body, and start building a gentler, more powerful inner voice.

That's something to celebrate.

Today is your checkpoint. A pause for reflection, integration, and gentle resetting before we move into the final, empowering phase of your healing journey.

Why Reflection Matters

Healing from anxiety isn't just about pushing forward. It's about stopping to see how far you've come.

When we reflect, we:

- Reinforce progress
- Recognize patterns
- Celebrate growth
- Adjust course gently, if needed

This isn't about being perfect. It's about *being present*—with yourself, your truth, and your journey.

A Look Back: What You've Covered So Far

Let's recap the ground you've covered:

- **Day 1**: You faced the truth about anxiety.
- **Day 2**: You understood the science behind it.
- **Day 3**: You began identifying your personal triggers.
- **Day 4**: You learned breathing and grounding tools.
- **Day 5**: You challenged negative thought patterns.
- **Day 6**: You improved your sleep, movement, and nutrition.

- **Day 7**: You reflected on Week One and reset.
- **Day 8**: You practiced mindfulness and presence.
- **Day 9**: You accepted your emotions without judgment.
- **Day 10**: You journaled for clarity and gratitude.
- **Day 11**: You set boundaries and protected your peace.
- **Day 12**: You reclaimed your sense of control.
- **Day 13**: You rewrote your self-talk with affirmations.

Let that sink in. That's powerful work.

Journal Prompt: Self-Assessment Check-In

Take some time today to answer the following prompts in your journal. Be honest and kind with yourself:

1. **What have I learned about my anxiety in the past two weeks?**
2. **What tools have helped me the most so far?**
3. **What moments this week made me feel proud, calm, or strong?**
4. **When did I feel most anxious this week? What triggered it? How did I respond?**

5. **What's something I'm still struggling with—and what's one small way I can support myself through it?**
6. **What is one thing I want to carry with me into Week 3?**

Affirmation Checkpoint

Which affirmations have you tried so far?

Which ones resonate most deeply?

If you haven't already, choose *one* to be your core mantra. Something you say every morning and night. Let it become your emotional anchor.

Examples:

- *"I am safe and grounded."*
- *"I trust myself to navigate life's ups and downs."*
- *"Peace is available to me in this moment."*

Write it on a sticky note. Keep it close.

Story: The Power of a Pause

Lena had always been an overachiever. She tackled her anxiety the same way—checklists, intense routines, constant pushing.

But she kept burning out.

On Day 14 of her healing journey, she did something new: *she paused.*

She sat on her balcony, journal in hand, and just... breathed. For the first time, she acknowledged how hard she'd been working—and how far she'd come.

That moment of stillness became the turning point. She realized healing wasn't about doing more. It was about being more *with* herself.

You don't need to do everything perfectly. You just need to keep showing up—and **pausing** when your soul asks for it.

Gentle Reset Tips for Week 3

As we prepare for the final stretch, here's how you can reset with intention:

1. Declutter Your Mind

Spend 10–15 minutes free-writing anything that's been cluttering your thoughts: worries, unfinished tasks, emotions you haven't processed.

Then... *close the journal.* You've released it.

2. Revisit Your Goals

What was your goal at the start of this journey? Managing panic attacks? Sleeping better? Feeling calmer?

Write a short letter to your future self describing how far you've come—and what you're committed to continuing.

3. Rebuild Your Routine

If you've fallen off your routine—no worries. That's part of the process.

This evening, map out a gentle, flexible plan for the next 7 days:

- Daily journal time
- 5 minutes of breathwork or mindfulness
- Repeat your affirmations
- Reflect on what works, and let go of what doesn't

Affirmations to Carry You Into Week 3

Here are a few powerful phrases to support the transition:

- *"I honor my progress, no matter how small."*
- *"Rest is part of my healing."*
- *"I trust the path I'm on."*
- *"I give myself permission to grow at my own pace."*

Repeat them daily. Let them root into your heart.

You're Doing Better Than You Think

We tend to underestimate our healing when we don't feel "100% better."

But healing doesn't always look dramatic. Sometimes it's subtle:

- Saying no without guilt
- Catching a negative thought before it spirals
- Sleeping a little better
- Showing up for yourself on a hard day

That's healing, too. And you're doing it.

Tomorrow's Focus: Building Confidence Through Action

Tomorrow begins Week 3—our final phase: *Empowerment and Growth*.

You'll learn how to build confidence through small, intentional actions that gently challenge your anxiety and expand your comfort zone.

For now, rest.

Reflect.

Reset.

You're ready for what's next.

Part III:

Creating Lasting Change (Days 15-21)

Empowerment and Growth

Day 15: Building Confidence Through Action

"Action is the antidote to fear." – Unknown

Welcome to the final phase of your healing journey — **Empowerment and Growth**.

Over the past 14 days, you've uncovered the roots of your anxiety, developed tools to manage it, and strengthened your emotional resilience. Now, it's time to take those internal shifts and bring them into your external world.

Today's focus is simple, yet powerful: **action**.

When anxiety takes over, it tricks us into avoidance — avoiding people, places, decisions, risks. Over time, this avoidance can shrink our lives and erode our confidence.

But confidence isn't something you wait to feel before taking action.

Confidence grows because you act — not the other way around.

Let's explore how taking small, brave actions can help you gently rebuild your sense of control, freedom, and confidence.

The Link Between Avoidance and Anxiety

Anxiety thrives in avoidance.

When we avoid something that makes us nervous — like public speaking, social situations, or confronting conflict — we get short-term relief.

But over time, the fear doesn't go away. It *grows.*

Our brains start to associate that situation with danger, reinforcing the idea that we *can't* handle it.

This is where **Exposure Therapy** comes in — a scientifically backed method for reducing anxiety by gradually facing our fears.

What Is Exposure Therapy (and How to Do It Safely)?

Exposure therapy isn't about throwing yourself into panic-inducing situations. It's about taking small, manageable steps to stretch your comfort zone and prove to your brain that you're safe.

Here's how to try it gently:

Step 1: Make a Fear Ladder

Write down something that makes you anxious. Then, break it into smaller steps, ranked from least to most anxiety-inducing.

Example: Fear of making phone calls

1. Listen to someone else make a call.
2. Call a friend or family member.
3. Call a store to ask their hours.
4. Call to book an appointment.
5. Answer an unknown number.

Start with the easiest. Repeat until your anxiety reduces. Then move to the next.

Step 2: Breathe and Anchor

Before and during each step, practice grounding techniques: deep breaths, positive self-talk, hand on your heart. Remind yourself: *"I am safe. I can do this."*

Step 3: Reflect

After completing each step, journal how it felt. Even if it was hard — **you did it.**

Story: Small Wins, Big Confidence

Jared had struggled with anxiety for years, especially around social events. His fear of embarrassment kept him isolated, stuck in his apartment.

When he began exposure therapy, his first step was simply walking into a coffee shop and ordering a drink. His hands shook. His voice cracked. But he survived.

That small win gave him the courage to try again — and again.

A month later, Jared gave a toast at his friend's birthday dinner.

Not because he *stopped* feeling anxious… but because he *proved* to himself that he could take action despite the fear.

That's real confidence.

Action Exercise: Your Confidence Challenge

Today, pick one small action that pushes you just a little outside your comfort zone.

Not a huge leap — a small stretch.

Examples:

- Send an email you've been avoiding.
- Speak up in a meeting or class.
- Go for a walk without checking your phone.
- Say "no" to something you don't want to do.
- Join an online forum or support group.

Before you do it, write this in your journal:

"Today, I choose courage over comfort. I trust myself to take this step."

Afterward, reflect:

- How did it feel?
- What did you learn?
- What would you say to yourself if you were your own coach?

Repeat this daily, if you can. **Small wins build strong confidence.**

Affirmations for Confidence and Courage

Repeat these aloud or write them in your journal:

- *"I am stronger than my anxiety."*
- *"Each small step I take builds my confidence."*
- *"I trust myself to handle what comes."*

- *"I can feel fear and move forward anyway."*

Say them even if you don't fully believe them yet. With repetition, your brain begins to accept them as truth.

Practical Tip: The 5-Second Rule

Sometimes anxiety keeps us stuck in overthinking. One powerful way to bypass this is using Mel Robbins' **5-Second Rule**:

When you feel the urge to act on a goal, count backward: *5... 4... 3... 2... 1 — GO.*

Then act. Make the call. Send the message. Speak up.

Counting down interrupts the anxiety loop and shifts your brain into action mode.

Try it today with your confidence challenge.

Journaling Prompts

Take time to explore the following questions:

1. What's one area of my life where I want to feel more confident?

2. What small actions can help me build that confidence?
3. What's one situation I've been avoiding due to fear?
4. What's the smallest, safest step I can take toward facing it?
5. How will I reward or celebrate myself afterward?

Let Go of the Myth of "Fearlessness"

You don't need to be fearless to be confident.

True confidence is feeling afraid… and choosing to act anyway.

You've already proven this over the past two weeks.

Now, you're strengthening it — day by day, step by step.

No need for perfection. Only progress.

Closing Reflection

Today's journey is about reclaiming your power through intentional, compassionate action.

Remember:

- You're not weak for feeling fear.
- You're brave for facing it.
- Every step matters — even the shaky ones.

You don't have to do big things to become confident.

You just have to keep doing *small brave things*, consistently.

Tomorrow, we'll talk about perfectionism — and how letting go of it can bring profound relief and freedom.

Day 16: Letting Go of Perfectionism

"Perfectionism is self-abuse of the highest order." – Anne Wilson Schaef

You're more than halfway through your healing journey.

By now, you've started taking small, courageous actions to reclaim your confidence. But today, we address one of anxiety's most subtle — and most toxic — fuel sources: **perfectionism**.

At first glance, perfectionism might look like a strength. High standards. Good results. Being polished and prepared.

But behind the shiny surface, perfectionism is a cage. A constant whisper of *"You're not enough."*

It doesn't inspire excellence — it breeds fear, shame, and paralysis.

Today, you'll learn how to break free from perfectionism and embrace the power of *"good enough."*

What Is Perfectionism (Really)?

Perfectionism isn't the same as striving for excellence.

It’s not about doing your best — it’s about fearing mistakes, rejection, or failure so much that it hijacks your happiness.

Some common signs of perfectionism:

- Procrastinating because you're afraid it won’t be perfect.
- Constantly doubting yourself or your work.
- Feeling like nothing you do is ever “good enough.”
- Avoiding new things because you might fail.
- Over-apologizing or over-preparing.
- Extreme fear of criticism or judgment.

Sound familiar?

Perfectionism keeps anxiety on high alert. Your brain is constantly scanning for flaws — and punishing you for not being “perfect.”

The Roots of Perfectionism

Most perfectionists didn’t choose to be that way.

Perfectionism is often rooted in early messages:

- *“I have to be perfect to be loved.”*
- *“Mistakes mean I’m a failure.”*
- *“If I’m not the best, I’m nothing.”*

These beliefs may have come from family, school, trauma, or societal pressures.

But here's the truth: **You are lovable and worthy exactly as you are. Not when you're perfect. Right now.**

Letting go of perfectionism isn't about becoming lazy — it's about becoming *free.*

Story: The Art of Imperfection

Sasha was a talented graphic designer. Her work was beautiful — but deadlines terrified her. She'd spend hours tweaking small details, starting over, obsessing over flaws no one else could see.

Her anxiety got so intense, she missed a few client projects. Her business began to crumble.

One day, her mentor said, "Sasha, done is better than perfect."

That sentence hit her like lightning.

She started turning in her projects at 90% — still good, but not paralyzed by perfection. To her surprise, her clients were thrilled. She began enjoying her work again — and sleeping better, too.

The day she embraced imperfection, she began to *heal.*

Exercise: Challenge the Inner Critic

Step 1: Write down a recent moment when you felt like what you did wasn't "good enough."

Step 2: Now, imagine your best friend did the exact same thing. What would you say to them?

Step 3: Write that down. Speak to yourself with that same compassion.

Your inner critic is not your truth. It's a scared part of you that needs love, not punishment.

Try This: The "Good Enough" Practice

Choose one task today that you would normally obsess over. A work project, email, outfit, cleaning, anything.

Do it **well enough**, then **stop**.

No re-checking ten times. No re-writing every word. Just finish it.

Say this aloud: *"This is good enough. I am good enough."*

This practice is uncomfortable at first. That's okay. You're retraining your brain to accept that **being human is better than being perfect.**

Affirmations to Let Go of Perfectionism

Speak or write the following:

- *"I release the need to be perfect."*
- *"My worth is not measured by my achievements."*
- *"Mistakes are part of growth, not proof of failure."*
- *"Done is better than perfect."*
- *"I choose progress over perfection."*

Repeat these anytime you feel yourself spiraling into over thinking or self-criticism.

Journaling Prompts

Take some time with these reflective questions:

1. Where in my life do I feel most pressure to be perfect?
2. What fears are hiding beneath that pressure?

3. How has perfectionism affected my mental health and relationships?
4. What would it look like to be "good enough" instead of perfect?
5. How can I celebrate my efforts, even if the result isn't flawless?

Practical Tips: Imperfect Is Powerful

Start before you're ready.
Perfectionism waits until everything is "just right." Action says: "Let's begin."

Set a time limit.
Give yourself a deadline and stick to it. Don't allow endless tweaking.

Celebrate mistakes.
Every mistake is proof you're trying, learning, growing. That's brave.

Speak it out loud.
When you catch yourself spiraling, say: *"This doesn't have to be perfect. I just need to show up."*

A Note for High Achievers

Letting go of perfectionism doesn't mean letting go of excellence.

It means redefining success:

- Not by the applause you get,
- But by the courage you show,
- And the peace you feel when you go to sleep at night.

True success is living in alignment with your values — not other people's expectations.

Closing Reflection

Perfectionism is just fear in a fancy outfit.

It tries to keep you safe — but instead, it keeps you small.

Today, choose to take up space.

Choose to be human.

Choose to breathe, create, share, speak, show up — even when it's messy.

You don't have to earn your worth through flawlessness.

You are already enough.

Exactly as you are.

Tomorrow, we'll explore how anxiety affects your relationships — and how to deepen your connection with others while protecting your peace.

Day 17: Deepening Relationships

"Anxiety does not empty tomorrow of its sorrows, but only empties today of its strength." – Charles Spurgeon

Anxiety often feels like a solitary struggle — but it rarely exists in isolation. It touches every part of our lives, including our **relationships**.

When anxiety becomes overwhelming, it can pull us inward. We withdraw, avoid vulnerability, or overanalyze every interaction. We fear judgment, rejection, or being a burden. And yet — we crave connection more than anything.

Today's chapter is about understanding how anxiety influences your relationships, and how to build stronger, more authentic connections — **without sacrificing your emotional well-being**.

Anxiety and Attachment

To understand how anxiety shows up in relationships, it helps to explore something called **attachment styles** — patterns developed in childhood that affect how we connect with others.

1. Secure Attachment

- Comfortable with closeness and independence.
- Communicates needs clearly.
- Can trust and be trusted.

2. Anxious Attachment

- Worries about being abandoned.
- Needs constant reassurance.
- Sensitive to shifts in tone or behavior.

3. Avoidant Attachment

- Values independence to the point of emotional distance.
- Struggles to express feelings.
- Withdraws when things feel intense.

Many people with anxiety lean toward anxious or avoidant patterns. You might:

- Obsess over texts, tone, or being "too much."
- Struggle with trust or vulnerability.
- Overthink social interactions after they've happened.

The good news? Awareness is the first step toward change.

Story: Breaking the Wall

Priya had always been seen as "the strong one" in her family and relationships. But under the surface, she was constantly over thinking — replaying conversations, worrying if people liked her, hiding her real emotions out of fear they'd push people away.

She kept people at a distance, always smiling, always agreeable.

But deep down, she felt alone.

In therapy, she realized that her anxiety wasn't just internal — it shaped how she showed up with others. She began practicing honesty in small ways. Saying "I'm feeling overwhelmed" instead of pretending everything was fine. Setting boundaries when needed.

The result?

Her relationships didn't fall apart. They deepened.

By showing up as her real self, Priya finally felt seen — and supported.

Practice: The Vulnerability Experiment

Vulnerability is scary. But it's the gateway to intimacy and connection.

Step 1: Think of one safe person in your life — a friend, family member, partner, or even a therapist.

Step 2: Choose one sentence to share that feels slightly vulnerable:

- "Lately I've been feeling anxious, and I'm not sure why."
- "Sometimes I worry I'll say the wrong thing."
- "I've been working on being more open — can I share something with you?"

Step 3: Share it. Then pause. Let them respond.

You don't need to share your whole story. Start small. Authenticity is magnetic — and healing.

Setting Boundaries Without Guilt

If vulnerability is one side of the coin, **boundaries** are the other.

Healthy boundaries are essential to protect your energy, reduce anxiety, and create safety in relationships.

Examples:

- "I'm not available to talk right now, but I'd love to check in later."
- "I need some time to myself this weekend to recharge."
- "I prefer not to talk about that topic."

Boundaries are not rejection. They are respect — for yourself and others.

Practice one small boundary today. Notice how your body feels afterward.

Affirmations for Connected, Peaceful Relationships

Repeat or write these:

- *"I am worthy of love and connection just as I am."*
- *"I can express my needs without guilt."*
- *"I attract relationships that feel safe and supportive."*
- *"My anxiety doesn't define my relationships."*
- *"It's safe for me to be seen."*

You are not "too much." You are not a burden. The right people will value the real you.

When Anxiety Causes Overthinking

One common relationship struggle with anxiety is **rumination** — replaying conversations, reading into silence, or assuming rejection without evidence.

Try this grounding technique:

1. **Name the thought**: "I'm assuming they're upset because they haven't replied."
2. **Check the facts**: "Is there proof? Or is this my anxiety talking?"
3. **Replace the story**: "They're probably just busy. I don't need to create a problem that doesn't exist."

You can also journal:

"Here's what I know for sure…"
"Here's what my anxiety is telling me…"
"Here's a more balanced thought…"

Journaling Prompts

Reflect on the following:

1. How has anxiety affected my relationships in the past?

2. What fears come up when I think about being vulnerable?
3. Who in my life feels emotionally safe?
4. What boundaries do I need to protect my peace?
5. What does a healthy, connected relationship look like to me?

A Note on Toxic Relationships

Not everyone in your life will be supportive. Some relationships may **intensify** your anxiety.

It's okay to outgrow people who make you feel small, unsafe, or drained.

Protecting your peace isn't selfish — it's survival.

If you need support in navigating toxic or abusive relationships, consider speaking with a licensed counselor or support group.

Closing Reflection

You deserve relationships that:

- Celebrate your growth.

- Hold space for your emotions.
- Respect your boundaries.
- Help you breathe easier — not harder.

As you heal, your relationships will shift. Some may fall away. Others will deepen. New ones will emerge.

Don't be afraid of this transformation.

When you show up as your full, authentic self — anxiety and all — you invite real love in.

Not love built on performance or perfection.

But love built on truth.

You are already worthy of it.

Tomorrow, we explore the digital world and how technology may be amplifying your anxiety — and what to do about it.

Day 18: Digital Detox and Mindful Tech Use

"Almost everything will work again if you unplug it for a few minutes — including you." – Anne Lamott

We live in a hyperconnected world. Phones buzz, emails ping, and the endless scroll of news and social media can feel like a vortex that never stops pulling us in. While technology brings convenience and connection, it also introduces **a constant stream of stimulation** — one that can quietly and steadily fuel anxiety.

Today's focus is about **taking back control**. It's time to step away from the noise, create mindful digital boundaries, and restore a sense of peace.

The Anxiety-Tech Connection

Studies have shown that excessive screen time — especially social media — is linked with increased anxiety, depression, sleep disturbances, and low self-esteem.

Here's why:

- **Information overload**: We're exposed to a non-stop feed of bad news, which can trigger chronic stress and hopelessness.

- **Comparison trap**: Social media often highlights people's best moments, creating unrealistic standards and feelings of inadequacy.
- **Disrupted sleep**: Blue light from screens interferes with melatonin production, impacting sleep quality — a key factor in anxiety.
- **Dopamine dependence**: Notifications trigger dopamine spikes, creating addictive loops of checking, refreshing, and needing constant stimulation.

Your brain — already sensitive due to anxiety — is trying to stay afloat in a digital flood.

Story: The Scroll Spiral

Raj was an early riser. But instead of starting his day with a peaceful routine, he grabbed his phone before even getting out of bed. Ten minutes of scrolling Instagram turned into an hour. He'd read five upsetting news stories, seen friends on vacation, and convinced himself that he wasn't doing enough in life.

By 9 a.m., his chest was tight, his heart raced, and his mind was full of comparison and dread. And the day hadn't even started.

A therapist challenged Raj to do a **24-hour phone detox**. No social media. No news. Just real life.

At first, he felt twitchy — like something was missing. But by the end of the day, he noticed something strange.

He felt calmer. Lighter. Clearer.

That was the moment Raj realized: *It wasn't just what he was thinking. It was what he was consuming.*

Practical Remedies for Digital Overload

Try one or more of these digital detox ideas today:

1. Morning Phone-Free Zone

Avoid screens for the first **30–60 minutes** after waking up. Replace with journaling, stretching, meditation, or simply sitting in silence.

2. Screen Time Audit

Check your phone's screen time stats. What apps consume most of your time? Are they adding or draining energy?

3. Set App Limits

Use app timers to cap usage. Try 20 minutes per day for social media, or uninstall apps entirely for a few days.

4. Tech-Free Evenings

Shut down screens at least an hour before bed. Replace with reading, a bath, light music, or talking to a loved one.

5. Digital Sabbath

Choose one day a week (or even a few hours) to go completely screen-free. Use that time to reconnect with nature, people, or yourself.

Affirmations for Digital Clarity

Repeat these aloud or write them in your journal:

- *"I choose what I consume with intention."*
- *"It's safe for me to disconnect."*
- *"I am present in my body and in this moment."*
- *"I am more than my notifications."*
- *"Unplugging is an act of healing."*

Mindful Social Media Use

If you're not ready for a full detox, try using social media **mindfully** instead of automatically.

Here's a simple 3-step approach:

1. **Pause before opening the app**. Ask: *Why am I opening this? What am I seeking?*
2. **Set a timer**. Give yourself 10-15 minutes, then log off.
3. **Reflect afterward**. How do you feel? Energized? Anxious? Empty? That feedback matters.

Also consider **curating your feed**:

- Un-follow accounts that make you feel "less than."
- Mute triggering content or toxic friends.
- Follow uplifting, educational, or calming pages.

Journaling Prompts

1. How do I usually feel after spending time online?
2. Which digital habits increase my anxiety?
3. What do I want more of in my offline life?
4. What boundaries can I set to protect my peace?
5. How can I use technology as a tool instead of a trap?

The Power of Being Present

The real gift of digital detoxing isn't just reducing anxiety. It's **reclaiming presence**.

You begin to notice:

- The way sunlight dances on your window.
- The warmth in a quiet cup of tea.
- The feeling of truly listening — or being heard.

These small moments often get lost in the digital blur. But they're where life actually happens.

Small Step: Your Digital Reset

Choose **one** of the following today:

✅ Turn off non-essential notifications.
✅ Delete one app for 24 hours.
✅ Go screen-free for the next two hours.
✅ Keep your phone in another room during meals.
✅ Do a "social scroll detox" after 8 p.m.

Pick just one. And pay attention to how you feel afterward.

Closing Reflection

You are not meant to be plugged in 24/7.

You are not a machine.

You are a human being with a nervous system that craves rhythm, stillness, and presence.

Technology can serve your healing — but only if **you** are in charge of it.

Today is your reminder that unplugging is not about missing out. It's about tuning in.

To your breath.
To your body.
To your life.

And that… is where peace lives.

Tomorrow, we'll explore Day 19: Spiritual and Creative Practices — connecting with something greater to heal anxiety from the soul outward.

Day 19: Spiritual and Creative Practices

"Art enables us to find ourselves and lose ourselves at the same time." – Thomas Merton

Healing anxiety isn't just about managing symptoms — it's about returning to wholeness. That wholeness often lives in spaces we overlook: **the spiritual and the creative.**

Whether it's prayer, art, music, nature, dance, or journaling, connecting to something **larger than yourself** — and something **within yourself** — can offer deep relief and resilience. Today is about exploring those sacred spaces.

What Is Spiritual Healing?

Spirituality doesn't have to mean religion. It simply means connecting with what gives your life **meaning, depth, and purpose**.

That might be:

- A belief in a higher power
- A connection to nature
- Practicing gratitude or presence

- The feeling of being part of something greater

Anxiety tends to shrink our perspective. It narrows our focus to fear, the future, and what might go wrong. But spiritual practice **expands** us — reminding us we are **not alone**, and that peace can be found even in uncertainty.

Story: Nature's Sanctuary

After years of battling panic attacks, Ayesha decided to try something unconventional. She began walking in the forest every morning — no headphones, no phone. Just trees, breath, and movement.

She didn't label it as spiritual. But soon, something shifted. The rustling leaves felt like whispers of comfort. The silence wasn't empty — it was full.

One day, after a walk, Ayesha realized something. "I don't feel anxious right now. I feel… alive."

That forest became her sanctuary. A place where her spirit could breathe.

Creative Practices as Healing Tools

Creating — in any form — has immense power to soothe an anxious mind. Why?

- **It shifts you into the present.** You can't worry about tomorrow while painting or singing.
- **It gives you expression.** Anxiety thrives in suppression. Creativity gives it voice.
- **It creates flow.** Flow states quiet the inner critic and activate calm.

You don't have to be an "artist" to benefit. You just have to be willing to try.

Here are a few healing creative practices to explore:

1. Art Journaling

Combine drawing, painting, or collage with written reflection. No rules. Just expression.

2. Music and Sound

Listen to calming music, create a playlist for your moods, or try playing an instrument — even banging a drum or humming a tune can be therapeutic.

3. Freewriting

Set a timer for 10 minutes and write without stopping. Let your subconscious speak.

4. Crafting

Knitting, gardening, pottery, cooking — all are forms of creation that offer grounding and satisfaction.

5. Movement

Try dance, yoga, or intuitive movement — anything that connects body to emotion.

Spiritual Practices to Anchor You

Anxiety often feels like floating. Spiritual practice can root you.

1. Prayer or Surrender

You can speak to a higher power, or simply say: *"I surrender what I cannot control."*

2. Meditation and Silence

Sit with yourself, breathe, and let stillness become your refuge.

3. Gratitude

List what you're thankful for — even small things. Gratitude grounds us in abundance, not fear.

4. Nature Connection

Go outside. Walk barefoot. Watch clouds. Touch a tree. Let nature's rhythm recalibrate you.

5. Ritual

Light a candle. Burn incense. Say a morning mantra. Rituals create sacred space and routine.

Affirmations for Spiritual and Creative Healing

- *"I trust in something greater than my fear."*
- *"My soul is safe to express itself."*
- *"Peace lives within me, and I can return to it."*
- *"My creativity is healing and sacred."*
- *"I allow beauty and meaning into my life."*

Repeat these in the mirror, write them down, or record them in your own voice.

Journaling Prompts

1. What does spirituality mean to me?
2. When was the last time I felt deeply connected to something bigger than myself?

3. What creative activity brings me joy or peace?
4. How can I make space for the sacred in my daily life?
5. If I trusted that I was being guided, how would I live differently?

Try This Today

Choose at least **one** of the following:

✅ Spend 15 minutes doing a creative activity with no outcome in mind.
✅ Take a walk in nature and observe with all five senses.
✅ Sit in stillness or prayer for 10 minutes.
✅ Create a mini altar with objects that bring you peace.
✅ Write a "letter to the universe" expressing your hopes, fears, or gratitude.

Let it be simple. Let it be yours.

Final Reflection

There is a part of you that anxiety cannot touch.

It's the part that sings when you paint, smiles when you see the sky, or feels warmth in silence. That part — your spirit — holds a quiet strength.

And the more you connect with it, the less power anxiety holds.

Today, you are invited to go inward and upward — to remember that you are more than your fears. You are a creator. A soul. A light.

Keep returning to that truth.

Tomorrow: Day 20 — Designing Your Post-21-Day Plan. You'll craft a sustainable healing routine to support your journey long after this book ends.

Day 20: Designing Your Post-21-Day Plan

"You do not rise to the level of your goals. You fall to the level of your systems." – James Clear

You've come a long way.

Over the past 19 days, you've faced your fears, explored your triggers, discovered calming tools, and learned to rewire your mind and body for peace. Today is about making sure this progress doesn't fade once the final page is turned.

This chapter is your **bridge** — from healing as a daily practice to healing as a way of life.

Let's design your post-21-day plan — a **sustainable system** to support you as you continue living with strength, clarity, and calm.

Why You Need a Long-Term Plan

Change doesn't stick just because we want it to. It sticks because we:

- Create systems that support our values.
- Build routines that remind us who we're becoming.

- Return to the tools that ground us.

Anxiety may still visit — but now you'll have a **toolbox**, not just wishful thinking.

Story: The Road Beyond the Retreat

After a 3-week anxiety recovery program, Leo felt better than ever. He had routines, clarity, and new confidence. But as life got busy again, he skipped journaling. Then stopped meditating. Slowly, his anxiety crept back.

One night during a panic attack, he pulled out the workbook from the program. On the last page, in his own handwriting, were five words: *"You know how to begin."*

He smiled. He did know. The work wasn't undone — it just needed reactivation.

Leo started small again. Within days, the fog began to lift.

Healing isn't a straight line — but it's always accessible.

Step 1: Define Your Essentials

Ask yourself: *What are the top 3 practices that help me feel centered, safe, and strong?*

Examples might include:

- Morning meditation or breathwork
- Daily journaling or gratitude list
- Evening walk or tech-free time
- Regular therapy or coaching
- Limiting caffeine or sugar
- Boundaries with work and social media

📓 **Write down your Top 3 essentials.** These are your **non-negotiables** — the core habits that anchor you.

Step 2: Build Your Daily/Weekly Rhythm

Create a simple schedule that supports your mental well-being.

Here's a sample:

Time of Day	Practice
Morning	10-min breath work, journal, tea
Afternoon	15-min walk or mindful break
Evening	Screen-free wind down, gratitude
Weekly	Sunday reflection, nature time

You don't need perfection. You need **consistency** — and flexibility. If you fall off, gently come back. That's strength.

Step 3: Design Your Personal Toolbox

Here's a structure for a powerful anxiety support toolbox:

□ **Calming Tools**

- Deep breathing
- Progressive muscle relaxation
- Grounding techniques (5-4-3-2-1 method)

□ **Cognitive Tools**

- Reframing thoughts
- Affirmations
- "What's true right now?" check-ins

❤□ **Emotional Tools**

- Journaling
- Talking to a friend or therapist
- Letting yourself cry or feel

❦ **Lifestyle Tools**

- Exercise or yoga
- Healthy eating habits
- Adequate sleep
- Limited alcohol or stimulant use

📌 **Write or print this toolbox** and keep it visible. Add your favorites from the last 20 days.

Step 4: Create Your "Rescue Plan"

Sometimes, anxiety hits hard. Instead of scrambling, build a **Rescue Plan** — a step-by-step guide to follow when you feel overwhelmed.

Example:

1. Pause and take 5 slow breaths.
2. Move to a safe space (bedroom, balcony, outdoors).
3. Use a grounding technique.
4. Write in journal: *What am I afraid of? What's actually happening?*
5. Call a trusted friend or coach.
6. Play calming music or use a meditation app.

Having this written plan can **interrupt panic** and provide structure during distress.

Step 5: Set Your Support System

No one heals alone.

- Who can you talk to when things get hard?
- Are you open to therapy, coaching, or a support group?

- Can you create a "check-in buddy" to text weekly?

❢ Consider writing a letter to your future self — offering support, reminders, and love when they may forget how strong they are.

Affirmations for Long-Term Resilience

- *"I am equipped to support myself every day."*
- *"My healing is ongoing, and that's okay."*
- *"I show up for myself with kindness and courage."*
- *"Even on tough days, I know what to do."*

Repeat these often — especially when doubt creeps in.

Journaling Prompts

1. What practices have helped me most during these 20 days?
2. What obstacles might challenge my routine — and how can I prepare for them?
3. How do I want to feel a month from now? What actions support that feeling?
4. What message does my present self want to give my future self?

Try This Today: Your Post-21 Plan

✅ Write out your daily mental health routine.
✅ List your top 3 essentials.
✅ Build your rescue plan.
✅ Create a "peace corner" at home — a space that reminds you to care for yourself.
✅ Reflect on how far you've come.

Final Reflection

You are no longer a beginner in this journey.

You are building a life — one grounded in awareness, compassion, and strength.

Healing is not a destination. It's a rhythm. A conversation. A relationship with yourself that you keep returning to.

There will be days you slip — and days you soar. But now, you have a map. A compass. A path.

And most importantly, you have **you** — wiser, stronger, and more equipped than ever.

Tomorrow is Day 21 — our final chapter: *Celebrate Your Healing Journey*. You'll honor your progress, write a letter to your future self, and close this chapter of deep healing with clarity and love.

Day 21: Celebrate Your Healing Journey

"The journey of healing is not about becoming someone new. It's about remembering who you were before the world taught you to be afraid." – Unknown

You've made it.

Day 21 isn't the end — it's a beginning. A renewal. A powerful moment to pause, reflect, and honor everything you've faced, felt, and transformed.

Today, we celebrate not just your commitment to healing — but your **courage**. Courage to face your fear. Courage to sit with discomfort. Courage to reclaim your peace.

Let's take a deep breath together.

You've done something extraordinary.

Your Journey, Day by Day

Look back at where you started. You may have begun with fear in your chest or doubt in your heart. You might have felt lost, overwhelmed, or stuck.

But through each chapter, you gathered tools, practiced new habits, rewrote limiting thoughts, and returned to yourself.

You've learned to:

- Face anxiety with awareness.
- Ground your body and calm your mind.
- Reflect through journaling.
- Embrace mindfulness and imperfection.
- Rebuild boundaries and confidence.
- Surrender control while reclaiming inner power.

Even on the days you struggled — you showed up.

That's healing.

Story: The Letter on the Mirror

After completing her 21-day anxiety healing plan, Meera didn't feel perfect — but she felt real.

She had tools. She had hope. She had herself.

On the final day, she wrote a letter to her future self and taped it to her mirror. It read:

"Dear Meera,
If you're reading this and feeling anxious again, please

remember:
You've walked through the storm before.
You have a breath. You have tools.
You are not broken.
You are healing, still. And that is beautiful."

Months later, on a hard day, Meera found the letter again. It was just what she needed.

Today, you'll write your letter, too.

Write a Letter to Your Future Self

This is your space — to encourage, affirm, and remind yourself of everything you've learned.

Start with:

- "Dear [Your Name],"
- Describe what you've accomplished in these 21 days.
- Share the tools that help you.
- Offer reassurance for the hard days.
- End with love and gratitude.

✍□ Take 10–15 minutes to write. Seal it in an envelope, place it in a journal, or post it somewhere special.

It will be your anchor in times of storm.

Affirmations to End This Journey

- *"I celebrate how far I've come."*
- *"I trust the process of my healing."*
- *"I am not my anxiety — I am so much more."*
- *"Every breath is a return to peace."*
- *"This is only the beginning of my freedom."*

Say them out loud. Write them. Let them live in you.

Journaling Prompts: Your Closing Reflection

1. What are the three most powerful things I've learned about myself during these 21 days?
2. What was the hardest day for me — and how did I get through it?
3. How do I now relate to my anxiety differently?
4. What new identity am I stepping into from this day forward?
5. What is my commitment to myself moving forward?

Ritual: Closing and Celebration

Take a moment to create a mini-closing ritual. This helps signal to your nervous system that a chapter is ending — and a new one is beginning.

Ideas:
✅ Light a candle or incense.
✅ Play a song that makes you feel empowered.
✅ Read your journal entries from the past 21 days.
✅ Take a walk in nature and say a quiet "thank you."
✅ Treat yourself to a meal, a bath, or something joyful.

Honor this chapter. Celebrate the **healer within you.**

You Are Not Your Anxiety

If there's one truth to carry forward, it is this:

Anxiety is an experience — not your identity.

You are the observer. The one who breathes through the storm. The one who asks for help. The one who reclaims their peace, over and over again.

You are resilient.

You are growing.

You are **enough.**

Progress Over Perfection

Healing isn't about never feeling anxious again.

It's about **responding** differently when anxiety arises.
It's about knowing where to turn, how to ground, when to rest.
It's about choosing yourself, again and again.

There will be days when you feel like you've regressed. That's normal.

But you now have proof: *You can find your way back.*

You've done it for 21 days.

You can do it again. As many times as you need.

You are **never alone.**

Final Words: Your Brave Heart

Dear Reader,

Thank you for showing up.
Thank you for facing the hard days.
Thank you for choosing healing.

This book may be ending, but your growth is just beginning. Keep learning. Keep breathing. Keep loving yourself, fiercely.

Whenever you feel anxious again, remember:
You have tools.
You have strength.
You have a roadmap.

Most of all…
You have **you.**

And that's more than enough.

With calm and courage,

We'd Love to Hear From You

Dear Reader,

Congratulations on completing your 21-day journey toward healing and peace. You've taken meaningful steps toward understanding and managing your anxiety, and that alone is something to be proud of. If this book, *Anxiety Therapy for men: Heal Yourself in 21 Days*, offered you hope, guidance, or comfort in any way, I kindly ask you to take a moment to leave a review.

Reviews help others discover this book. They also let me know that the message and tools shared here have made a difference. Just a few words — whether about a chapter you connected with, a tool you used, or an insight you gained — can truly inspire someone else to start their healing journey.

You can leave your review by going to the book's page on Amazon and clicking the **"Write a customer review"** button.

Thank you for being part of this journey. Your healing matters, and so does your voice.

With warmth and gratitude,

Abhijit-Sharma

More From the Author: International Best Seller

TRAIN YOUR
BRAIN
TO BE
HAPPY
21 days life changing exercises on How to be Happy
Writer
ABHIJIT SHARMA

www.ingramcontent.com/pod-product-compliance
Lightning Source LLC
Chambersburg PA
CBHW050016170726
48282CB00025B/424
* 9 7 8 9 3 3 4 3 1 7 7 4 9 *